Graph-Based Methods for Natural Language Processing Workshop 2017 (TextGraphs-11)

AA001990

Held at ACL 2017

Vancouver, Canada
3 August 2017

ISBN: 978-1-5108-4574-9

Printed from e-media with permission by:

Curran Associates, Inc.
57 Morehouse Lane
Red Hook, NY 12571

Some format issues inherent in the e-media version may also appear in this print version.

Copyright© (2017) by the Association for Computational Linguistics
All rights reserved.

Printed by Curran Associates, Inc. (2017)

For permission requests, please contact the Association for Computational Linguistics
at the address below.

Association for Computational Linguistics
209 N. Eighth Street
Stroudsburg, Pennsylvania 18360

Phone: 1-570-476-8006
Fax: 1-570-476-0860

acl@aclweb.org

Additional copies of this publication are available from:

Curran Associates, Inc.
57 Morehouse Lane
Red Hook, NY 12571 USA
Phone: 845-758-0400
Fax: 845-758-2633
Email: curran@proceedings.com
Web: www.proceedings.com

TextGraphs-11

**Graph-Based Methods for
Natural Language Processing**

Proceedings of the Workshop

August 3, 2017
Vancouver, Canada

©2017 The Association for Computational Linguistics

Introduction to TextGraphs-11

Welcome to TextGraphs, the workshop on Graph-based Methods for Natural Language Processing. The eleventh edition of the workshop is being organized on August 3, 2017, in conjunction with the 55th Annual Meeting of the Association for Computational Linguistics (ACL-2017), being held in Vancouver in Canada.

For the past eleven years, the workshops in the TextGraphs series have published and promoted the synergy between the field of Graph Theory (GT) and Natural Language Processing (NLP). The target audience of our workshop has comprised of researchers working on problems related to either Graph Theory or graph-based algorithms applied to Natural Language Processing, social media, and the Semantic Web.

The TextGraphs workshop series addresses a broad spectrum of research areas within NLP. This is because, besides traditional NLP applications like parsing, word sense disambiguation, semantic role labeling, and information extraction, graph-based solutions also target web-scale applications like information propagation in social networks, rumor proliferation, e-reputation, language dynamics learning, and future events prediction, to name a few. Following this tradition, this year's TextGraphs also presents research from diverse topics such as semantics, word embeddings, text coherence, multilingual applications and summarization.

Previous editions of TextGraphs have featured special themes, such as "Cognitive and Social Dynamics of Languages in the framework of Complex Networks" and "Large Scale Lexical Acquisition and Representation". For TextGraphs 2017, we set a special focus on the usage of graph-based methods to interpret deep learning models for NLP tasks. Though deep learning models have displayed state-of-the-art performance on many NLP tasks, they are often criticized for not being interpretable (due to their various layers and large number of parameters). Through our theme, we hoped to spur a discussion on the development of methods for reasoning and interpretation of the layers used in deep learning models, given that a neural network is, from one point of view, nothing but a graph.

We are pleased to have two excellent invited speakers for this year's event. We thank Apoorv Agarwal and Michael Strube for their enthusiastic acceptance of our invitation. We also thank Verisk for sponsoring an invited speaker and the best paper award. Finally, we are thankful to the members of the program committee for their valuable and high quality reviews. All submissions have benefited from their expert feedback. Their timely contribution was the basis for accepting an excellent list of papers and making this edition of TextGraphs a success.

Martin Riedl, Swapna Somasundaran, Goran Glavaš and Ed Hovy
TextGraphs-11 Organizers
July 2017

Organizers:

Martin Riedl, Univeristät Hamburg, Germany
Swapna Somasundaran, Educational Testing Service, Princeton, USA
Goran Glavaš, University of Mannheim, Germany
Eduard Hovy, Carnegie Mellon University, USA

Program Committee:

Alan Akbik, Zalando, Germany
Sivaji Bandyopadhyay, Jadavpur University, Kolkata, India
Chris Biemann, Univeristät Hamburg, Germany
Pushpak Bhattacharyya, IIT Bombay, India
Tomáš Brychcín, University of West Bohemia, Czech Republic
Tanmoy Chakraborty, University of Maryland, USA
Monojit Choudhury, Microsoft Research, India
Asif Ekbar, Indian Institute of Technology, Patna, India
Stefano Faralli, University of Mannheim, Germany
Michael Flor, Educational Testing Services, USA
Marc Franco Salvador, University of Valencia, Spain
Tomáš Hercig, University of West Bohemia, Czech Republic
Ioana Hulpus, University of Mannheim, Germany
Roman Klinger, University of Stuttgart, Germany
Nikola Ljubešić, University of Zagreb, Croatia
Héctor Martínez Alonso, Inria & University Paris Diderot, France
Gabor Melli, VigLink, USA
Rada Mihalcea, University of Michigan, USA
Alessandro Moschitti, University of Trento, Italy
Animesh Mukherjee, IIT Kharagpur, India
Vivi Nastase, Fondazione Bruno Kessler, Italy
Roberto Navigli, "La Sapienza" University of Rome, Italy
Alexander Panchenko, Univeristät Hamburg, Germany
Simone Paolo Ponzetto, University of Mannheim, Germany
Steffen Remus, Univeristät Hamburg, Germany
Stephan Roller, UT Austin, USA
Shourya Roy, Xerox Research, India
Josef Steinberger, University of West Bohemia, Czech Republic
Anders Søgaard, University of Copenhagen, Denmark
Jan Šnajder, University of Zagreb, Croatia
Kateryna Tymosenko, University of Trento, Italy
Aline Villavicencio, F. University of Rio Grande do Sul, Brazil
Ivan Vulić, University of Cambridge, United Kingdom
Fabio Massimo Zanzotto, "Tor vergata" University of Rome, Italy

Invited Speakers:

Apoorv Agarwal, Columbia University, USA
Michael Strube, HITS gGmbH, Heidelberg, Germany

Sponsor:

Verisk Analytics

Table of Contents

Conference Program

Thursday, August 3, 2017

9:00–9:10   *Opening remarks*
Swapna Somasundaran and Goran Glavaš

9:10–10:10   *Invited talk: How communication networks inform interpretation of language*
Apoorv Agarwal

10:10–10:30   *On the "Calligraphy" of Books*
Vanessa Queiroz Marinho, Henrique Ferraz de Arruda, Thales Sinelli, Luciano da Fontoura Costa and Diego Raphael Amancio

10:30–11:00   Coffee break

11:00–11:20   *Adapting predominant and novel sense discovery algorithms for identifying corpus-specific sense differences*
Binny Mathew, Suman Kalyan Maity, Pratip Sarkar, Animesh Mukherjee and Pawan Goyal

11:20–11:40   *Merging knowledge bases in different languages*
Jerónimo Hernández-González, Estevam R. Hruschka Jr. and Tom M. Mitchell

11:40–12:00   *Parameter Free Hierarchical Graph-Based Clustering for Analyzing Continuous Word Embeddings*
Thomas Alexander Trost and Dietrich Klakow

12:00–12:15   *Spectral Graph-Based Method of Multimodal Word Embedding*
Kazuki Fukui, Takamasa Oshikiri and Hidetoshi Shimodaira

12:15–14:00   Lunch

14:00–15:00   *Invited talk*
Michael Strube

15:00–15:15   *Graph Methods for Multilingual FrameNets*
Collin Baker and Michael Ellsworth

15:15–15:30   *Extract with Order for Coherent Multi-Document Summarization*
Mir Tafseer Nayeem and Yllias Chali

15:30–16:00   *Coffee break*

16:00–16:20   *Work Hard, Play Hard: Email Classification on the Avocado and Enron Corpora*
Sakhar Alkhereyf and Owen Rambow

16:20–16:40   *A Graph Based Semi-Supervised Approach for Analysis of Derivational Nouns in Sanskrit*
Amrith Krishna, Pavankumar Satuluri, Harshavardhan Ponnada, Muneeb Ahmed, Gulab Arora, Kaustubh Hiware and Pawan Goyal

16:40–17:00   *Evaluating text coherence based on semantic similarity graph*
Jan Wira Gotama Putra and Takenobu Tokunaga

17:00–17:10   *Best paper award and closing remarks*
Swapna Somasundaran and Goran Glavaš

On the "Calligraphy" of Books

Vanessa Queiroz Marinho*   Henrique Ferraz de Arruda*   Thales Sinelli Lima*
Luciano da Fontoura Costa†   Diego Raphael Amancio*
*Institute of Mathematics and Computer Science, University of São Paulo, Brazil
†São Carlos Institute of Physics, University of São Paulo, Brazil
Corresponding authors: {vanessa.qm.1,diegoraphael}@gmail.com

Abstract

Authorship attribution is a natural language processing task that has been widely studied, often by considering small order statistics. In this paper, we explore a complex network approach to assign the authorship of texts based on their mesoscopic representation, in an attempt to capture the flow of the narrative. Indeed, as reported in this work, such an approach allowed the identification of the dominant narrative structure of the studied authors. This has been achieved due to the ability of the mesoscopic approach to take into account relationships between different, not necessarily adjacent, parts of the text, which is able to capture the story flow. The potential of the proposed approach has been illustrated through principal component analysis, a comparison with the chance baseline method, and network visualization. Such visualizations reveal individual characteristics of the authors, which can be understood as a kind of calligraphy.

1   Introduction

The ever increasing availability of public content on the Internet – including books, tweets, and blog posts – has implied in many new developments in several natural language processing (NLP) areas such as machine translation, sentiment analysis, and authorship attribution. Recently, advancements in the latter task have been achieved by using complex networks (Antiqueira et al., 2006; Amancio et al., 2011; Lahiri and Mihalcea, 2013; Marinho et al., 2016; Akimushkin et al., 2017).

The network models used in many of these works are based on word co-occurrence. In this approach, each distinct word is represented by a node, and edges connect adjacent words. Although this networked representation has proven successful in many tasks, it is not without its share of problems. Co-occurrence networks do not portray the topical structure found in many texts and are usually devoid of community structure (de Arruda et al., 2016). In order to overcome this disadvantage, some techniques have been devoted to the *mesoscopic* representation of texts (de Arruda et al., 2016, 2017). de Arruda et al. (2017) proposed a novel networked model, in which each node represents a respective set of consecutive paragraphs, while weighted edges express the similarity between nodes. Their proposed network is able to extract the organization and flow of text by effectively capturing the similarity between the blocks of text. In addition, their method was employed to distinguish between real and shuffled texts. However, mesoscopic networks have not been applied to tackle other NLP tasks.

Most researchers in the field of authorship attribution assume that each author has a signature (known as authorial fingerprint) that distinguishes his/her writing from the others (Juola, 2006). So inspired, we decided to test the hypothesis that these authorial fingerprints are also visible at a mesoscopic scale. At this scale, distinctive graphical patterns of the course of the text emerge, akin to a "discourse calligraphy" of the author. Thus, in order to classify texts according to their authorship, we created mesoscopic networks from texts and employed a set of topological measurements. In particular, the main goal of this paper is to probe whether the authors' writing styles correlate with the story flow of their books.

This paper is structured as follows: Section 2 briefly describes the problem and some complex network approaches for authorship attribu-

1

Proceedings of TextGraphs-11: the Workshop on Graph-based Methods for Natural Language Processing, ACL 2017, pages 1–10,
Vancouver, Canada, August 3, 2017. ©2017 Association for Computational Linguistics

tion. The process to create mesoscopic networks is explained in Section 3. In addition, we also describe the dataset, the selected measurements and the machine learning algorithms in Section 3. The obtained results are reported in Section 4. Finally, Section 5 outlines our conclusions and prospects for future work.

2 Related Work

Authorship attribution methods attempt to find the most likely author of a document (Stamatatos, 2009). Since the seminal work conducted by Mosteller and Wallace (1964), authorship attribution has been a widely studied problem and several different approaches have been proposed. One of the first approaches consisted in analyzing the frequency of common words, such as *to* or *the*, in order to classify political essays according to their authorship (Mosteller and Wallace, 1964).

Since then, Mosteller and Wallace (1964)'s method has been enhanced to incorporate different attributes capable of qualifying writing styles. These include lexical, character, syntactic, and semantic features (Stamatatos, 2009). Simple lexical and character features (e.g. frequency and burstiness of words and characters, average lengths of texts, and others) have been used in several works, as reported by Grieve (2007), Koppel et al. (2009), and Stamatatos (2009). Most of these works have achieved good results by using, for example, the frequency of stopwords. Examples of syntactic information include the frequencies of POS tags and constituency-based parsing tree rules (Baayen et al., 1996; Gamon, 2004; Hirst and Feiguina, 2007). Finally, semantic features can be extracted from semantic dependency graphs and from the semantic roles associated with some words (Gamon, 2004; Argamon et al., 2007).

The usage of network analysis in authorship attribution has already been studied from different perspectives. Antiqueira et al. (2006), one of the first works in the area, extracted some measurements from co-occurrence networks and discovered that these could be used to characterize the writing style of authors. Amancio et al. (2011) combined network measurements with the distribution of words to characterize the authorship of several books. Lahiri and Mihalcea (2013) carried out an in-depth authorship attribution study using more than 100 features extracted from co-occurrence networks. They found that local fea-

tures (those extracted from individual nodes) outperform global features in the authorship attribution problem.

Apart from using traditional network measurements, the frequency of network motifs involving three nodes (Milo et al., 2002) was found useful to characterize the writing style (Marinho et al., 2016). Instead of considering the text as a static structure, Akimushkin et al. (2017) studied the topology evolution of co-occurrence networks extracted from different sections of the text. Unlike most of the previous mentioned works, in which stopwords are usually removed, Segarra et al. (2013) proposed an authorship attribution method based on networks formed only by stopwords.

3 Methods

In this section, we describe the process to create mesoscopic networks from raw texts. We also detail the network measurements and machine learning methods.

3.1 Mesoscopic Approach

There are several ways to represent texts as complex networks, such as co-occurrence, syntactic, semantic or similarity networks (Mihalcea and Radev, 2011; Cong and Liu, 2014). In this study, we adopt the mesoscopic network approach proposed by de Arruda et al. (2017). Such networks are able to represent the text unfolding along time, which is normally overlooked by traditional approaches. Moreover, these networks were used to classify documents between real and shuffled texts, using only simple statistics. The high accuracy rate obtained in that classification task led us to infer that mesoscopic networks are able to represent structural aspects of real texts, such as the organization and development of the author's idea.

In order to create the network from a given text (T), some preprocessing steps can be applied. In our study, we removed the stopwords, and the remaining words were lemmatized. Figure 1 illustrates the methodology used to create mesoscopic networks. In the first step, shown in Figure 1(a), the text is partitioned into a set of paragraphs, $T = (p_0, p_1, p_2, \cdots)$, where p_i is a sequence of the preprocessed words belonging to the same paragraph i. Different from the co-occurrence networks, where nodes represent words, in mesoscopic networks nodes encompass sequences of Δ consecutive paragraphs. More

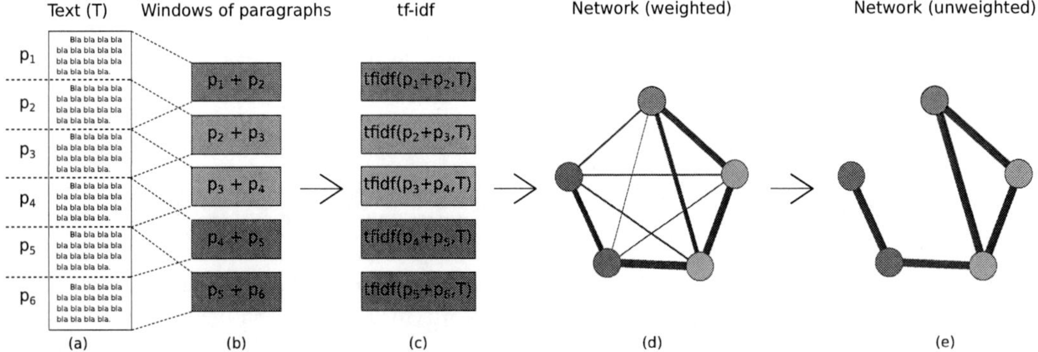

Figure 1: Illustration of the mesoscopic approach proposed by de Arruda et al. (2017). First, the text T is divided into subsequent paragraphs (a). Overlapping windows with $\Delta = 2$ paragraphs are shown in (b). Then, the tf-idf map is computed for all windows (c). Each pair of nodes (windows) i and j is now connected by an edge, weighted by the cosine similarity between their respective tf-idf maps (d). Next, in the network pruning phase, the edges with the lowest weights are removed until the network reaches a given average degree $\langle k \rangle$. The network in (e) illustrates the obtained unweighted mesoscopic network with $\langle k \rangle = 2$.

specifically, each possible subsequent set with Δ paragraphs, $W_i^\Delta = (p_i, p_{i+1}, \cdots, p_{i+\Delta-1})$, represents a network node, as shown in Figure 1(b).

So as to account for the importance of the words in a given paragraph, we applied the *tf-idf* (Manning and Schütze, 1999) statistics, which was originally proposed to quantify the importance of a given word w in a document d given a corpus D. A tf-idf(w, d, D) map is computed as

$$\text{tf-idf}(w, d, D) = \frac{f_{w,d}}{n} \times \log\left(\frac{|D|}{d_w}\right), \quad (1)$$

where $f_{w,d}$ is the frequency of word w in the document d, n is the total number of words in the document d, $|D|$ represents the total number of documents and d_w is the number of documents in which w occurs at least once. In order to apply the tf-idf measurement, we considered all the possible windows of subsequent paragraphs, W_i^Δ, as the set of documents D (see Figure 1(c)). Finally, for each pair of nodes i and j, a respective edge is created and its weight is calculated according to the cosine similarity between tf-idf(W_i^Δ, T) and tf-idf(W_j^Δ, T), where tf-idf(W_i^Δ, T) is a tf-idf vector of all words, computed from a given set of paragraphs W_i^Δ. This step is illustrated in Figure 1(d).

In order to convert the network from weighted to unweighted, the edges with the lowest weights can be removed, as described in Section 3.2. It should be noted that edges originating from adja-

cent paragraphs tend to have higher weights because of the implied overlap. Figure 1(e) shows an example of unweighted network. In our experiment, we set $\Delta = 20$, as empirically determined elsewhere (de Arruda et al., 2017).

3.2 Network Pruning

Mesoscopic networks are complete weighted graphs, i.e. every node is connected to every other node (Newman, 2010). In this paper, we repeatedly removed the edges with the lowest weights until each network reached a fixed network average degree $\langle k \rangle$. The average degree of a network g, with E edges and N nodes, is defined as

$$\langle k \rangle = \frac{2 * E}{N}. \quad (2)$$

We used several values of $\langle k \rangle$, ranging from 5 to 50, by steps of 5.

3.3 Network Measurements

The following network measurements were extracted from the networks[1]. Most of these measurements (apart from assortativity) apply to a single node. So, in order to obtain more global characterization, we calculated the average, standard deviation and skewness (third moment) of each distribution. The obtained statistics from these distributions were then used as features in the machine learning methods.

---

[1] For most of these measurements, we used the Igraph software package (Csardi and Nepusz, 2006)

Degree: The degree quantifies the number of connections of a node (Costa et al., 2007). Even though the average degree of all networks is the same as a consequence of network pruning, the degree of each node may still vary inside the network. Therefore, we used the standard deviation and skewness of this measurement, disregarding the average.

Average Degree of Neighbors: The average degree of neighbors (Pastor-Satorras et al., 2001) quantifies how well connected are the neighbors of a node.

Assortativity: As described by Newman (2003), the assortativity quantifies how likely it is for a given node to connect to other nodes with similar degree. Lower than zero values of assortativity are obtained when a node tends to connect to others with very different degrees. When a node connects only to others with the same degree, the assortativity becomes one. Null assortativity indicates that there is no correlation.

Clustering Coefficient: This measurement reflects how well interconnected are the neighbors of a given node (Watts and Strogatz, 1998).

Accessibility $(h = \{2, 3\})$: The accessibility of a node i is based on Shannon's entropy (Shannon and Weaver, 1963) of the probability of accessing nodes at the hth concentric level, centered at i, by a given dynamics starting at that node (Travençolo and Costa, 2008). Here, we adopted the self-avoiding random walk as the reference dynamics.

Symmetry $(h = \{2, 3, 4\})$: This measurement (Silva et al., 2016b), obtained for each node i, quantifies the symmetry of the topology around i. It can be understood as a normalization of the accessibility, and includes two components: *backbone*, where edges between nodes from the same concentric level are discarded, and *merged*, where nodes that share edges in the same level are merged.

Network visualization can provide means to better understand the structure of a given book's story by organizing, into an embedding space, the topology of the obtained network. We applied a visualization methodology based on force-directed graph drawing (Silva et al., 2016a). Specifically, this method is based on the Fruchterman and Reingold (1991) (FR) algorithm, which simulates a system of particles, which attract and repel one another. The attractive force, f_a, reflects the node connectivity, while the repulsive force, f_r, acts between all pair of nodes. A gravitational force, f_g, can also be added. We adopted $f_a = 0.0002$, $f_r = 1.25$, and $f_g = 0.001$.

3.4 Machine Learning Methods

Several classifiers — Decision Trees, Random Forest, kNN, Logistic Regressors, SVM, Naive Bayes (Duda et al., 2000) — were tested in order to choose the most adequate. Support Vector Machines (SVM) and Random Forest were selected. We used the Linear SVM implementation (with default parameters), and Random Forest with 50 trees, both available at *Scikit-learn* (Pedregosa et al., 2011). We employed the *leave-one-out* cross-validation technique, in which only one dataset instance is used as test while all the others are taken for training the classifier. Feature selection was attempted, but no particular subset of features stood out. Therefore, all measurements were considered.

4 Results and Discussion

In this section, we describe the selected dataset and present the obtained results organized in two parts: (i) the complete set of authors; and (ii) four authors representing major types of works.

4.1 Dataset

In order to investigate whether authors can be distinguished by the story flow in their works, we created mesoscopic networks from several texts. Our dataset is composed of 100 English texts written by 20 distinct authors (five texts per author) extracted from Machicao et al. (2016). The selected 20 authors are: Andrew Lang, Arthur Conan Doyle, B. M. Bower, Bram Stoker, Charles Darwin, Charles Dickens, Edgar Allan Poe, H. G. Wells, Hector H. Munro (Saki), Henry James, Herman Melville, Horatio Alger, Jane Austen, Mark Twain, Nathaniel Hawthorne, P. G. Wodehouse, Richard Harding Davis, Thomas Hardy, Washington Irving, and Zane Grey. The whole dataset was obtained from the Project Gutenberg repository[2]. The complete list of used texts is available at this link [3].

4.2 Complete Set of Authors

In the first experiment, we used all the books by all 20 authors, yielding the results presented in Ta-

[2]Project Gutenberg - https://www.gutenberg.org/
[3]https://goo.gl/2pJJHG

ble 1. Remarkably, though the chance baseline for this experiment is only 5% (each author has the same probability of being randomly selected), our best result was as high as 35%. Moreover, 17 (48.5%) out of the 35 books correctly classified by our method were written by only 4 authors: namely Andrew Lang, B. M. Bower, Hector H. Munro (Saki), and Henry James

Table 1: Accuracy rate in discriminating the authorship of texts.

Average Degree	Random Forest	SVM
$\langle k \rangle = 5$	10%	12%
$\langle k \rangle = 10$	18%	14%
$\langle k \rangle = 15$	22%	25%
$\langle k \rangle = 20$	25%	24%
$\langle k \rangle = 25$	21%	17%
$\langle k \rangle = 30$	21%	23%
$\langle k \rangle = 35$	16%	17%
$\langle k \rangle = 40$	16%	23%
$\langle k \rangle = 45$	18%	25%
$\langle k \rangle = 50$	16%	20%
All combined	26%	**35%**

We also performed a pairwise classification. The obtained results were compared with a traditional approach usually employed in the literature, the analysis of the most frequent words. For this experiment, we used the original texts of each book, extracted the frequency of the 20 most frequent words, and then used a SVM classifier. Figure 2 shows the accuracies for the traditional features, and Figure 3 illustrates the pairwise classification accuracies when mesoscopic networks were used to model each text, we did not select a single average degree $\langle k \rangle$, but rather we combined all the degrees listed in Table 1. The accuracies were obtained with the SVM classifier.

A careful examination of Figure 2 and 3 reveals that for some cases, except the squares with lighter colors, our results are on par with those obtained with the frequency of the 20 most frequent words (mainly stopwords). Moreover, our method even achieved higher accuracies in some combinations. See, for example, authors Grey and Munro, for which 7 and 6, respectively, of our results were better than the traditional approach. One thing that we should note, and which will be revisited in the following subsection, is the fact that it is hard for mesoscopic networks to distinguish Edgar Allan Poe from Charles Darwin. In this case, we obtained an accuracy rate of 50%, contrasted to 80% achieved by the other approach.

4.3 Small Set of Authors

Out of the 20 authors considered in the previous subsection, we selected four authors, namely Charles Darwin, Thomas Hardy, Edgar Allan Poe, and Mark Twain. They were chosen because two of them have several *novels* (Thomas Hardy and Mark Twain), Edgar Allan Poe is best known for writing *short stories* and Charles Darwin wrote about his *scientific theories* and observations. The now obtained accuracy rate in classifying them was enhanced to 65% (Random Forests) and 50% (SVM) by using the mesoscopic representation, contrasted to the chance baseline of 25% obtained for four authors. The Principal Component Analysis (PCA) (Jolliffe, 2002) considering these four authors is presented in Figure 4.

The PCA results indicate a clear partitioning between the groups of books associated to each author. Remarkably, one of Thomas Hardy's book (*A Changed Man and Other Tales*) resulted between those of Edgar Allan Poe and Charles Darwin. Such a good partitioning is a consequence of the quite different mesoscopic networks obtained for these authors, as depicted in Figure 5.

The mesoscopic networks presented in Figure 5 unveil interesting aspects, including an unexpected similarity to intricate calligraphic shapes. Note that the books which contain tales or short stories, such as those by Edgar Allan Poe, as well as the book *A Changed Man and Other Tales*, present a similar chain-like topology with a few cycles. Moreover, most of these cycles appear at a relatively small scale. Interestingly, the scientific books of Charles Darwin also present this chain-like structure, which is probably related to the nature of his writings, describing his theories, observations, and findings.

It is clear, visually, that the other books present more complex stories, where paragraphs (nodes) from different parts of the book sharing similar content resulted in intersections. For example, the book *Adventures of Huckleberry Finn* tells the story of Huckleberry Finn traveling down the Mississippi river. During most of the book, he goes through different small adventures along the river. Another interesting point is that this book ends in a similar setting as it begins, when Huckleberry Finn returns to his city, which is reflected in the

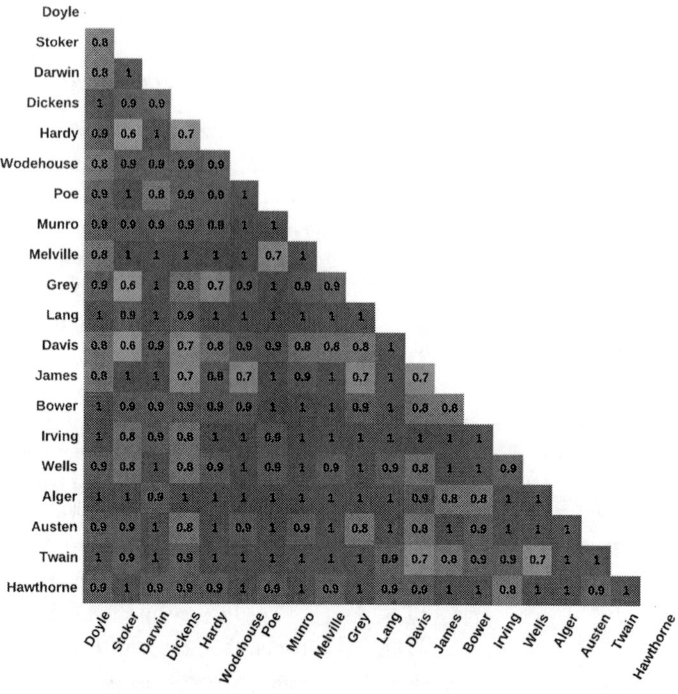

Figure 2: Accuracy rate (from 0 to 1) in the pairwise classification using the frequency of the 20 most frequent words.

respective return of the unfolding trajectory to its beginning. It is important to highlight that a full visual analysis with all the 20 authors was beyond the scope of this experiment. Our primary goal was to perform a preliminary investigation of the books through geometrical approaches.

5 Conclusion

Complex network methods have been applied with growing success to several natural language processing tasks. In some of these approaches, a chunk of text is represented as a co-occurrence network, which reflects the syntactic relationship between words (Cancho and Solé, 2001). Although this is a well-known representation, it is not without its share of problems. Those networks, for example, are unable to represent the topical structure found in many texts. So as to overcome such a limitation, a mesoscopic representation has been recently proposed (de Arruda et al., 2017). The main goal of that approach was to take into account the semantical relationship between chunks of text. More specifically, the network nodes correspond to texts from consecutive paragraphs, while the edges are weighted by the similarity between the respective texts. Statistics of some local topological measurements were used to characterize books' mesoscopic networks. We tested the hypothesis that such a representation is useful at assigning the authorship to documents. In particular, we advocated that fingerprints left by each author are visible at a mesoscopic scale.

The obtained accuracy rates, which in one case surpassed by 40 percentage points the chance baseline, suggest that the proposed approach is capable of revealing writing styles characteristics. In addition, we performed an alternative classification, in which all pairs of distinct authors were considered. In some cases our method provided better results than those obtained with traditional features. Such a result indicates that features obtained from mesoscopic networks can be used as a complement to more traditional features of texts. In order to better understand the unfolding of texts, we selected authors whose works include short stories, novels, and scientific writing. A set of topological features was estimated and PCA projected. Interestingly, in this projected space, a

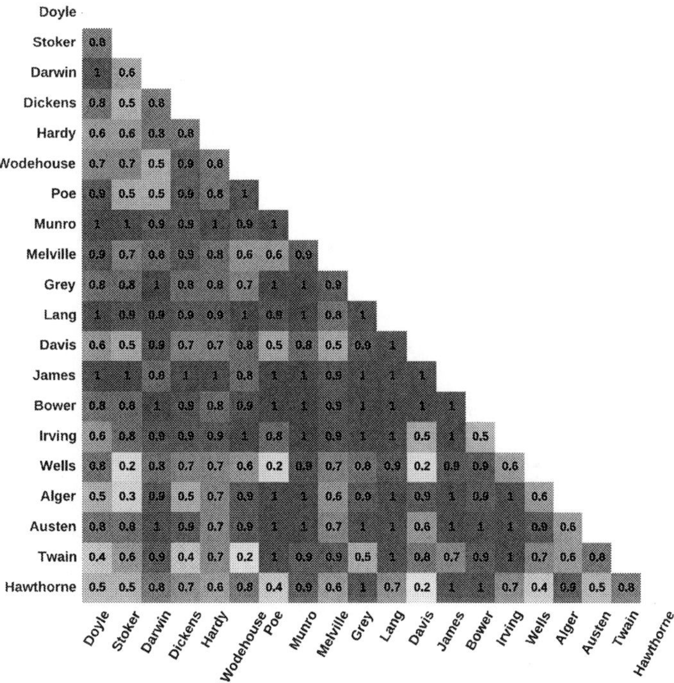

Figure 3: Accuracy rate (from 0 to 1) in the pairwise classification using network features extracted from mesoscopic networks.

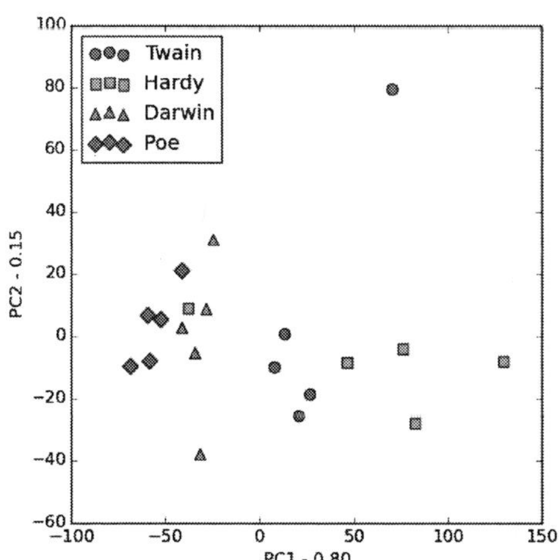

Figure 4: PCA of the books written by Charles Darwin, Thomas Hardy, Edgar Allan Poe, and Mark Twain.

book of tales written by *Thomas Hardy* resulted closer to *Edgar Allan Poe*'s books, which are also composed of short stories. Even more surprising, the patterns obtained by the visualization resulted quite representative of the different types of works, suggesting a "calligraphy". Such visualizations reveal intricate discourse patterns in the books.

The goal of this paper was not to provide state-of-the-art results for authorship attribution, given that most traditional approaches in the literature have achieved results as high as 90% (Grieve, 2007; Koppel et al., 2009). Instead, we report an approach that can be used to obtain novel stylometric features, as well as to complement traditional methods.

Future works could apply a similar approach to other related tasks — such as authorship verification, plagiarism detection, and topic segmentation — and also extend the mesoscopic representation to include different granularity levels, such as sentences or chapters. Another possibility is to investigate the relationship between the emotional content of a text and its topology.

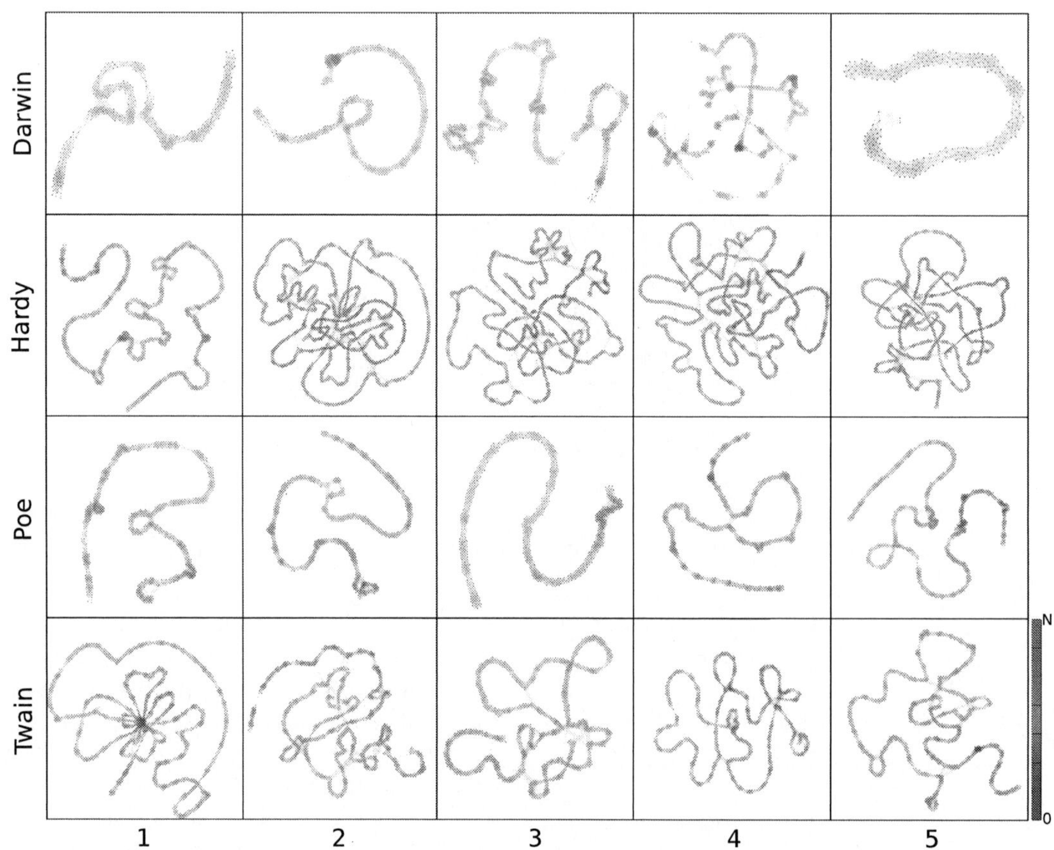

Figure 5: Mesoscopic networks for 20 books of four different authors. **Charles Darwin:** (1) *Coral Reefs*, (2) *The Expression of the Emotions in Man and Animals*, (3) *Geological Observations on South America*, (4) *The Different Forms of Flowers on Plants of the Same Species*, and (5) *Volcanic Islands*. **Thomas Hardy:** (1) *A Changed Man; and Other Tales*, (2) *A Pair of Blue Eyes*, (3) *Far from the Madding Crowd*, (4) *Jude the Obscure*, and (5) *The Hand of Ethelberta*. **Edgar Allan Poe:** *The Works of Edgar Allan Poe - Volume (1) to (5)*. **Mark Twain:** (1) *Adventures of Huckleberry Finn*, (2) *The Adventures of Tom Sawyer*, (3) *The Prince and the Pauper*, (4) *A Connecticut Yankee in King Arthur's Court*, and (5) *Roughing It*. The bluish nodes represent the windows formed by paragraphs from the beginning of the book and the greenish ones represent the windows formed by paragraphs from the end of the book. The order of the windows can be seen in the legend, where N represents the last window.

Acknowledgments

V.Q.M. and D.R.A. acknowledge financial support from São Paulo Research Foundation (FAPESP) (grant no. 15/05676-8, 16/19069-9). H.F.A. and T.S.L. thank CAPES for financial support. L.d.F.C. is grateful to CNPq (Brazil) (grant no. 307333/2013-2), FAPESP (grant no. 11/50761-2), and NAP-PRP-USP for sponsorship.

References

C. Akimushkin, D. R. Amancio, and O. N. Oliveira Jr. 2017. Text authorship identified using the dynamics of word co-occurrence networks. *PLoS ONE* .

D. R. Amancio, E. G. Altmann, O. N. Oliveira Jr, and L. F. Costa. 2011. Comparing intermittency and network measurements of words and their dependence on authorship. *New Journal of Physics.* 13(12):123024.

L. Antiqueira, T. A. S. Pardo, M. G. V. Nunes, O. N. Oliveira Jr, and L. F. Costa. 2006. Some issues on complex networks for author characterization. In *Fourth Workshop in Information and Human Language Technology in the Proceedings of International Joint Conference IBERAMIA-SBIA-SBRN*. ICMC-USP, Ribeirão Preto, Brazil.

S. Argamon, C. Whitelaw, P. Chase, S. R. Hota, N. Garg, and S. Levitan. 2007. Stylistic text classification using functional lexical features. *Journal of the American Society for Information Science and Technology* 58(6):802–822.

H. Baayen, H. van Halteren, and F. Tweedie. 1996. Outside the cave of shadows: using syntactic annotation to enhance authorship attribution. *Literary and Linguistic Computing* 11(3):121.

R. F. i Cancho and R. V. Solé. 2001. The small world of human language. *Proceedings of The Royal Society of London. Series B, Biological Sciences* 268:2261–2266.

J. Cong and H. Liu. 2014. Approaching human language with complex networks. *Physics of life reviews* 11(4):598–618.

L. da F. Costa, F. A. Rodrigues, G. Travieso, and P. R. Villas Boas. 2007. Characterization of complex networks: A survey of measurements. *Advances in physics* 56(1):167–242.

G. Csardi and T. Nepusz. 2006. The igraph software package for complex network research. *InterJournal* Complex Systems:1695.

H. F. de Arruda, L. da F. Costa, and D. R. Amancio. 2016. Topic segmentation via community detection in complex networks. *Chaos: An Interdisciplinary Journal of Nonlinear Science.* 26(6).

H. F. de Arruda, F. N. Silva, V. Q. Marinho, D. R. Amancio, and L. da F. Costa. 2017. Representation of texts as complex networks: a mesoscopic approach. *arXiv preprint arXiv:1606.09636v2* .

R. O. Duda, P. E. Hart, and D. G. Stork. 2000. *Pattern Classification (2nd Edition)*. Wiley-Interscience.

T. M. J. Fruchterman and E. M. Reingold. 1991. Graph drawing by force-directed placement. *Software: Practice and experience* 21(11):1129–1164.

M. Gamon. 2004. Linguistic correlates of style: authorship classification with deep linguistic analysis features. In *Proceedings of International Conference on Computational Linguistics (COLING)*. Geneva, Switzerland, pages 611–617.

J. Grieve. 2007. Quantitative authorship attribution: An evaluation of techniques. *Literary and Linguistic Computing* 22(3):251.

G. Hirst and O. Feiguina. 2007. Bigrams of syntactic labels for authorship discrimination of short texts. *Literary and Linguistic Computing* 22(4):405–417.

I. Jolliffe. 2002. *Principal component analysis*. Wiley Online Library.

P. Juola. 2006. Authorship attribution. *Foundations and Trends in Information Retrieval* 1(3):233–334.

M. Koppel, J. Schler, and S. Argamon. 2009. Computational methods in authorship attribution. *Journal of the American Society for Information Science and Technology.* 60(1):9–26.

S. Lahiri and R. Mihalcea. 2013. Authorship attribution using word network features. *arXiv preprint arXiv:1311.2978* .

J. Machicao, E. A. Correa Jr., G. H. B. Miranda, D. R. Amancio, and O. M. Bruno. 2016. Authorship attribution based on life-like network automata. *arXiv preprint arXiv:1610.06498* .

C. D. Manning and H. Schütze. 1999. *Foundations of Statistical Natural Language Processing*. MIT Press, Cambridge, MA, USA.

V. Q. Marinho, G. Hirst, and D. R. Amancio. 2016. Authorship attribution via network motifs identification. In *Proceedings of the 5th Brazilian Conference on Intelligent Systems (BRACIS)*. Recife, Brazil.

R. Mihalcea and D. Radev. 2011. *Graph-based natural language processing and information retrieval*. Cambridge University Press, Cambridge; New York.

R. Milo, S. Shen-Orr, S. Itzkovitz, N. Kashtan, D. Chklovskii, and U. Alon. 2002. Network motifs: simple building blocks of complex networks. *Science* 298(5594):824–827.

F. Mosteller and D. L. Wallace. 1964. *Inference and Disputed Authorship: The Federalist Papers*. Addison-Wesley, Reading, Mass.

M. Newman. 2003. Mixing patterns in networks. *Physical Review E* 67(2):026126.

M. Newman. 2010. *Networks: An Introduction.* Oxford University Press, Inc., New York, NY, USA.

R. Pastor-Satorras, A. Vázquez, and A. Vespignani. 2001. Dynamical and correlation properties of the Internet. *Physical Review Letters* 87(25):258701.

F. Pedregosa, G. Varoquaux, A. Gramfort, V. Michel, B. Thirion, O. Grisel, M. Blondel, P. Prettenhofer, R. Weiss, V. Dubourg, et al. 2011. Scikit-learn: Machine learning in python. *Journal of Machine Learning Research.* 12(Oct):2825–2830.

S. Segarra, M. Eisen, and A. Ribeiro. 2013. Authorship attribution using function words adjacency networks. In *International Conference on Acoustics, Speech and Signal Processing (ICASSP).* IEEE, pages 5563–5567.

C. E. Shannon and W. Weaver. 1963. *A Mathematical Theory of Communication.* University of Illinois Press, Champaign, IL, USA.

F. N. Silva, D. R. Amancio, M. Bardosova, L. da F. Costa, and O. N. Oliveira Jr. 2016a. Using network science and text analytics to produce surveys in a scientific topic. *Journal of Informetrics.* 10(2):487–502.

F. N. Silva, C. H. Comin, T. K. DM. Peron, F. A. Rodrigues, C. Ye, R. C. Wilson, E. R. Hancock, and L. da F. Costa. 2016b. Concentric network symmetry. *Information Sciences* 333:61–80.

E. Stamatatos. 2009. A survey of modern authorship attribution methods. *Journal of the American Society for Information Science and Technology.* 60(3):538–556.

B. A. N. Travençolo and L. da F. Costa. 2008. Accessibility in complex networks. *Physics Letters A* 373(1):89–95.

D. J. Watts and S. H. Strogatz. 1998. Collective dynamics of small-worldnetworks. *Nature* 393(6684):440–442.

Adapting predominant and novel sense discovery algorithms for identifying corpus-specific sense differences

Binny Mathew[1], Suman Kalyan Maity[2], Pratip Sarkar[3]
Animesh Mukherjee[4] and Pawan Goyal[5]
Department of Computer Science and Engineering
Indian Institute of Technology Kharagpur, India - 721302
Email: {binny.iitkgp[1], pratip.sarkar.iitkgp[3], animeshm[4], pawang.iitk[5]}@gmail.com
sumankalyan.maity@cse.iitkgp.ernet.in[2]

Abstract

Word senses are not static and may have temporal, spatial or corpus-specific scopes. Identifying such scopes might benefit the existing WSD systems largely. In this paper, while studying corpus specific word senses, we adapt three existing predominant and novel-sense discovery algorithms to identify these corpus-specific senses. We make use of text data available in the form of millions of digitized books and newspaper archives as two different sources of corpora and propose automated methods to identify corpus-specific word senses at various time points. We conduct an extensive and thorough human judgment experiment to rigorously evaluate and compare the performance of these approaches. Post adaptation, the output of the three algorithms are in the same format and the accuracy results are also comparable, with roughly **45-60%** of the reported corpus-specific senses being judged as genuine.

1 Introduction

Human language is neither static not uniform. Almost every individual aspect of language including phonological, morphological, syntactic as well as semantic structure can exhibit differences, even for the same language. These differences can be influenced by a lot of factors such as time, location, corpus type etc. However, in order to suitably understand these differences, one needs to be able to analyze large volumes of natural language text data collected from diverse corpora. It is only in this Big Data era that unprecedented amounts of text data have become available in the form of millions of digitized books (Google Books project),

newspaper documents, Wikipedia articles as well as tweet streams. This huge volume of time and location stamped data across various types of corpora now allows us to make precise quantitative linguistic predictions, which were earlier observed only through mathematical models and computer simulations.

Scope of a word sense: One of the fundamental dimensions of language change is shift in word usage and word senses (Jones, 1986; Ide and Veronis, 1998; Schütze, 1998; Navigli, 2009). A word may possess many senses; however, not all of the senses are used uniformly; some are more common than the others. This particular distribution can be heavily dependent on the underlying time-period, location or the type of corpora. For example, let us consider the word "rock". In books, it is usually associated with the sense reflected by the words 'stone, pebble, boulder' etc., while if we look into newspapers and magazines, we find that it is mostly used in the sense of 'rock music'.

Motivation for this work: The world of technology is changing rapidly, and it is no surprise that word senses also reflect this change. Let us consider the word "brand". This word is mainly used for the 'brand-name' of a product. However, it has now become a shorthand reference to the skills, actions, personality and other publicly perceived traits of individuals or for characterizing reputation, public face of the whole group or companies. The rise of social media and the ability to self-publish and self-advertise undoubtedly led to the emergence of this new sense of "brand". To further motivate such cross corpus sense differences, let us consider the word 'relay'. A simple Google search in the News section produces results that are very different from those obtained through a search in the Books section (See Fig 1). In this paper, we attempt to automatically build corpus-specific contexts of a target word (for e.g., relay in

Proceedings of TextGraphs-11: the Workshop on Graph-based Methods for Natural Language Processing, ACL 2017, pages 11–20,
Vancouver, Canada, August 3, 2017. ©2017 Association for Computational Linguistics

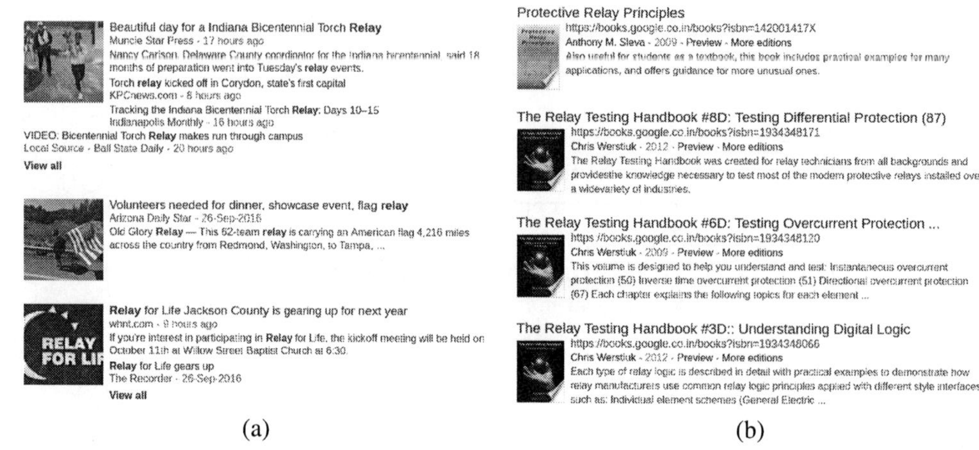

Figure 1: Google search results for the word 'relay' using (a) Google News and (b) Google Books.

this case) that can appropriately discriminate the two different senses of the target word – one of which is more relevant for the News corpus (context words extracted by one of our adapted methods: *team, race, event, races, sprint, men, events, record, run, win*) while the other is more relevant for the Books corpus (context words extracted by one of our adapted methods: *solenoid, transformer, circuitry, generator, diode, sensor, transistor, converter, capacitor, transformers*). Since the search engine users mostly go for generic search without any explicit mention of book or news, the target word along with a small associated context vector might help the search engine to retrieve document from the most relevant corpora automatically. We believe that the target and the automatically extracted corpus-specific context vector can be further used to enhance (i) semantic and personalized search, (ii) corpora-specific search and (iii) corpora-specific word sense disambiguation. It is an important as well as challenging task to identify predominant word senses specific to various corpora. While the researchers have started exploring the temporal and spatial scopes of word senses (Cook and Stevenson, 2010; Gulordava and Baroni, 2011; Kulkarni et al., 2015; Jatowt and Duh, 2014; Mitra *et al.*, 2014; Mitra *et al.*, 2015), corpora-specific senses have remained mostly unexplored.

Our contributions: Motivated by the above applications, this paper studies corpora-specific senses for the first time and makes the following contributions [1] : (i) we take two different methods for novel sense discovery (Mitra *et al.*, 2014; Lau *et al.*, 2014) and one for predominant sense identification (McCarthy *et al.*, 2004) and adapt these in an automated and unsupervised manner to identify corpus-specific sense for a given word (noun), and (ii) perform a thorough manual evaluation to rigorously compare the corpus-specific senses obtained using these methods. Manual evaluation conducted using 60 candidate words for each method indicates that $\sim$**45-60%** of the corpus-specific senses identified by the adapted algorithms are genuine. Our work is a unique contribution since it is able to adapt three very different types of major algorithms suitably to identify corpora specific senses.

Key observations: For manual evaluation of the candidate corpus-specific senses, we focused on two aspects – a) *sense representation*, which tells if the word cluster obtained from a method is a good representative of the target word, and b) *sense difference*, which tells whether the sense represented by the corpus-specific cluster is different from all the senses of the word in the other corpus. Some of our important findings from this study are: (i) the number of candidate senses produced by McCarthy *et al.* (2004) is far less than the two other methods, (ii) Mitra *et al.* (2014) produces the best representative sense cluster for a word in the time period 2006-2008 and McCarthy *et al.* (2004) produces the best representative sense cluster for a word in the time period 1987-1995, (iii) Mitra *et al.* (2014) is able to identify sense differences more accurately in comparison to the other methods, (iv) considering both the aspects together, McCarthy *et al.* (2004) performs the best, (v) for

---

[1]The code and evaluation results are available at: `http://tinyurl.com/h4onyww`

the common results produced by Lau *et al.* (2014) and Mitra *et al.* (2014), the former does better sense differentiation while the latter does better overall.

2 Related Work

Automatic discovery and disambiguation of word senses from a given text is an important and challenging problem, which has been extensively studied in the literature (Jones, 1986; Ide and Veronis, 1998; Schütze, 1998; Navigli, 2009; Kilgarriff and Tugwell, 2001; Kilgarriff, 2004). Only recently, with the availability of enormous amounts of data, researchers are exploring temporal scopes of word senses. Cook and Stevenson (2010) use corpora from different time periods to study the change in the semantic orientation of words. Gulordava and Baroni (2011) use two different time periods in the Google n-grams corpus and detect semantic change based on distributional similarity between word vectors. Kulkarni *et al.* (2015) propose a computation model for tracking and detecting statistically significant linguistic shifts in the meaning and usage of words. Jatowt and Duh (2014) propose a framework for exploring semantic change of words over time on Google n-grams and COHA dataset. Lau *et al.* (2014) propose a fully unsupervised topic modelling-based approach to sense frequency estimation, which was used for the tasks of predominant sense learning, sense distribution acquisition, detecting senses which are not attested in the corpus, and identifying novel senses in the corpus which are not captured in the sense inventory. Two recent studies by Mitra *et al.* (2014; 2015) capture temporal noun sense changes by proposing a graph clustering based framework for analysis of diachronic text data available from Google books as well as tweets. quantify semantic change by evaluating word embeddings against known historical changes. Lea and Mirella (2016) develop a dynamic Bayesian model of diachronic meaning change. Pelevina (2016) develops an approach which induces a sense inventory from existing word embeddings via clustering of ego-networks of related words.

Cook *et al.* (2013) induce word senses and then identify novel senses by comparing two different corpora: the 'focus corpora' (i.e., a recent version of the corpora) and the 'reference corpora' (older version of the corpora). Tahmasebi *et al.* (2011), propose a framework for tracking senses in a newspaper corpus containing articles between 1785 and 1985. Phani *et al.* (2012) study 11 years worth Bengali newswire that allows them to extract trajectories of salient words that are of importance in contemporary West Bengal. Few works (Dorow and Widdows, 2003; McCarthy *et al.*, 2004) have focused on corpus-specific sense identification. Our work differs from these works in that we capture the cross corpus-specific sense differences by comparing the senses of a particular word obtained across two different corpora. We adapt three state-of-the-art novel and predominant sense discovery algorithms and extensively compare their performances for this task.

3 Dataset Description

To study corpora-specific senses, we consider books and newspaper articles as two different corpora sources. We compare these corpora for the same time-periods to ensure that the sense differences are obtained only because of the change in corpus and not due to the difference in time. A brief description of these datasets is given below.

Books dataset: The books dataset is based on the Google Books Syntactic n-grams corpus (Goldberg and Orwant, 2013), consisting of time-stamped texts from over 3.4 million digitized English books, published between 1520 and 2008. For our study, we consider Google books data for the two time periods $1987-1995$ and $2006-2008$.

Newspaper dataset: For the Newspaper dataset, we consider two different data sources. The first dataset from $1987-1995$ contains articles of various newspapers[2]. The other dataset from $2006-2008$ is gathered from the archives of The New York Times.

4 Proposed framework

To identify corpus-specific word senses, we aim at adapting some of the existing algorithms, which have been utilized for related tasks. In principle, we compare all the senses of a word in one corpus against all the senses of the same word in another corpus. We, therefore, base this work on three different approaches, Mitra *et al.* (2014), Lau *et al.* (2014) and McCarthy *et al.* (2004), which could be adapted to find word senses in different corpora in an unsupervised manner. Next, we discuss these methods briefly followed by the pro-

---

[2]https://catalog.ldc.upenn.edu/LDC93T3A

posed adaptation technique and generation of the candidate set.

4.1 Mitra's Method

Mitra *et al.* (2014) proposed an unsupervised method to identify noun sense changes over time. They prepare separate distributional-thesaurus-based networks (DT) (Biemann and Riedl, 2013) for the two different time periods. Once the DTs have been constructed, Chinese Whispers (CW) algorithm (Biemann, 2006) is used for inducing word senses over each DT. For a given word, the sense clusters across two time-points are compared using a split-join algorithm.

Proposed adaptation: In our adaptation, we apply the same framework but over the two different corpora sources in the same time period. So, for a given word w that appears in both the books and newspaper datasets, we get two different set of clusters, B and N, respectively for the two datasets. Accordingly, let $B = \{s_{b1}, s_{b2}, \ldots, s_{b|B|}\}$ and $N = \{s_{n1}, s_{n2}, \ldots, s_{n|N|}\}$, where s_{bi} (s_{nj}) denotes a sense cluster for w in the books (news) dataset.

A corpus-specific sense will predominantly be present only in that specific corpus and will be absent from the other corpus. To detect the book-specific sense for the word w, we compare each of the $|B|$ book clusters against all of the $|N|$ newspaper clusters. Thus, for each cluster s_{bi}, we identify the fraction of words that are not present in any of the $|N|$ newspaper clusters. If this value is above a threshold, we call s_{bi} a book-specific sense cluster for the word w. This threshold has been set to 0.8 for all the experiments, as also reported in Mitra *et al.* (2014).

We also apply the multi-stage filtering[3] to obtain the candidate words as mentioned in their paper, except that we do not filter the top 20% and bottom 20% of the words. We believe that removing the top 20% words would deprive us of many good cases. To take care of the rare words, we consider only those corpus-specific clusters that have ≥ 10 words .

The number of candidate words obtained after this filtering are shown in Table 1. Figure 2 (a,b) illustrates two different sense clusters of the word 'windows' - one specific to books corpus and another specific to newspaper corpus, as obtained us-

---

[3]majority voting after multiple runs of CW and POS tags 'NN' and 'NNS'

ing Mitra's method. The book-specific sense corresponds to 'an opening in the wall or roof of a building'. The newspaper-specific sense, on the other hand, is related to the computing domain, suggesting Windows operating system.

Table 1: Number of candidate corpus-specific senses using Mitra's method after multi-stage filtering

	1987-1995	2006-2008
Books	32036	30396
Newspapers	18693	20896

4.2 McCarthy's Method

McCarthy et. al. (2004) developed a method to find the predominant sense of target word w in a given corpora. The method requires the nearest neighbors to the target word, along with the distributional similarity score between the target word and its neighbors. It then assigns a prevalence score to each of the WordNet synset ws_i of w by comparing this synset to the neighbors of w. The prevalence score PS_i for the synset ws_i is given by

$$PS_i = \sum_{n_j \in N_w} dss(w, n_j) \times \frac{wnss(ws_i, n_j)}{\sum_{ws_{i'}} wnss(ws_{i'}, n_j)} \quad (1)$$

where N_w denotes the set of neighbors of w and $dss(w, n_j)$ denotes the distributional similarity between word w and its neighbors n_j. $wnss(ws_i, n_j)$ denotes the WordNet similarity between the synset ws_i and the word n_j, and is given by

$$wnss(ws_i, n_j) = \max_{ns_x \in senses(n_j)} ss(ws_i, ns_x)$$
$$(2)$$

where $ss(ws_i, ns_x)$ denotes the semantic similarity between WordNet synsets ws_i and ns_x. We use Lin Similarity measure to find similarity between two WordNet synsets.

Proposed adaptation: In our adaptation to McCarthy's method to find corpus-specific senses, we use the DT networks constructed for Mitra's method to obtain the neighbors as well as distributional similarity between a word and its neighbors. We then obtain the prevalence score for each sense of the target word for both the corpora sources separately, and normalize these scores so that the scores add up to 1.0 for each corpus. We call these as normalized prevalence score (NPS).

We call a sense ws_i as corpora specific if its NPS_i is greater than an upper threshold in one

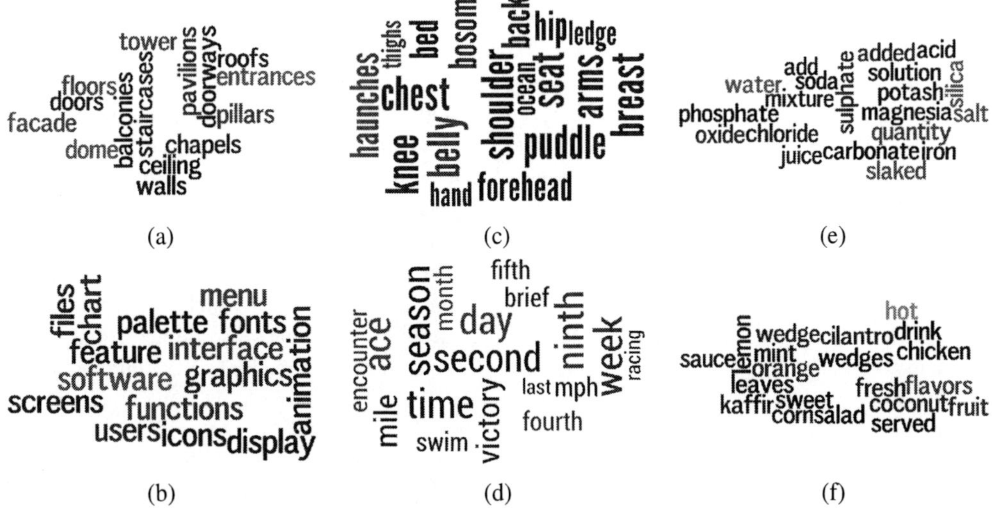

Figure 2: Examples of corpora-specific sense clusters obtained for (a,b) 'windows' using Mitra's method for (books, news) during 1987-1995, (c,d) 'lap' using McCarthy's method for (books, news) during 2006-2008 and (e,f) 'lime' using Lau's method for (books, news) during 2006-2008.

corpus and less than a lower threshold in the other corpus. We use 0.4 as the upper threshold and 0.1 as the lower threshold for our experiments. After applying this threshold, the number of candidate words are shown in Table 2.

Table 2: Number of candidate corpus-specific senses using McCarthy's method.

	1987-1995	2006-2008
Books	97	95
Newspapers	117	97

For the purpose of distributional visualization of the senses, we denote a word sense ws_i using those neighbors of the word, which make the highest contribution to the prevalence score PS_i. Figure 2 (c, d) illustrates two sense clusters of the word 'lap' thus obtained - one specific to books corpus and another specific to newspaper corpus. The book-specific sense corresponds to 'the top surface of the upper part of the legs of a person who is sitting down'. The news-specific sense, on the other hand corresponds to 'a complete trip around a race track that is repeated several times during a competition'.

4.3 Lau's Method

We also adapt the method described in Lau *et al.* (2014) to find corpus specific word senses. Their method uses topic modeling to estimate word sense distributions and is based on the word sense induction (WSI) system described in Lau *et*

al. (2012). The system is built around a Hierarchical Dirichlet Process (HDP) (Teh *et al.*, 2006), which optimises the number of topics in a fully-unsupervised fashion over the training data. For each word, they first induce topics using HDP. The words having the highest probabilities in each topic denote the sense cluster. The authors treat the novel sense identification task as identifying sense clusters that do not align well with any of the pre-existing senses in the sense inventory. They use topic-to-sense affinity to estimate the similarity of a topic to the set of senses given as

$$ts - affinity(t_j) = \frac{\sum_i^S Sim(s_i, t_j)}{\sum_l^T \sum_k^S Sim(s_k, t_l)} \quad (3)$$

where T and S represent the number of topics and senses respectively, and $Sim(s_i, t_j)$ is defined as

$$Sim(s_i, t_j) = 1 - JS(S_i || T_j) \quad (4)$$

where S_i and T_j denote the multinomial distributions over words for sense s_i and topic t_j. $JS(X, Y)$ stands for Jensen-Shannon divergence between distributions X and Y.

Proposed adaptation: In our adaptation to their method to find corpus-specific senses, for a target word, a topic is called corpus-specific if its word distributions are very different from all the topics in the other corpus. We therefore compute similarity of this topic to all the topics in other corpus and if the maximum similarity is below a threshold, this topic is called as corpus-specific. We use

Equation 4 to compute the similarity between two topics t_i and t_j as $Sim(t_i, t_j)$.

Since Lau's method is computationally expensive to run over the whole vocabulary, we run it only for those candidate words, which were flagged by Mitra's method. We then use a threshold to select only those topics which have low similarity to all the topics in the other corpus. We use 0.35 as the threshold for all the 4 cases except for news-specific senses in 2006-2008, where a threshold of 0.2 was used. The number of candidate corpus-specific senses thus obtained are shown in Table 3. Note that a word may have multiple corpus-specific senses.

Table 3: Number of candidate words using Lau's method.

	1987-1995	2006-2008
Books	6478	4339
Newspapers	23587	1944

Figure 2(e,f) illustrates the two different word clusters of the word 'lime' - one specific to the books corpus and another specific to the newspaper corpus, as obtained by applying their method. The book-specific sense corresponds to 'mineral and industrial forms of calcium oxide'. The news-specific sense, on the other hand, is related to 'lemon, lime juice'.

5 Evaluation Framework and Results

In this section, we discuss our framework for evaluating the candidate corpus-specific senses obtained from the three methods. We perform manual evaluations using an online survey[4] among $\sim$ 27 agreed participants (students, researchers, professors, technical persons) with age between 18-34 years. We randomly selected 60 candidate corpus-specific senses (combining both corpora sources) from each of the three methods (roughly 30 words from each time period). Each participant was given a set of 20 candidate words to evaluate; thus each candidate sense was evaluated by 3 different annotators. In the survey, the candidate word was provided with its corpus-specific sense cluster (represented by word-clouds of the words in the cluster) and all the sense clusters in the other corpus.

Questions to the participants: The participants were asked two questions. First, *whether the candidate corpus-specific sense cluster is a good representative sense of the target word?* and second, *whether the sense represented by the corpus-specific cluster is different from all the senses of the word in the other corpus?* The participants could answer the first question as 'Yes' or 'No' and this response was taken as a measure of "sense representation" accuracy of the underlying scheme. If this answer is 'No', the answer to the second response was set as 'NA'. If this answer is 'Yes', they would answer the second question as 'Yes' or 'No', which was taken as a measure of "discriminative sense detection" accuracy of the underlying method for comparing the senses across the two corpora. The overall confidence of a method was obtained by combining the two responses, i.e., whether both the responses are 'Yes'. The accuracy values are computed using *majority voting*, where we take the output as 'Yes' if majority of the responses are in agreement with the system and *average accuracy*, where we find the fraction of responses that are in agreement with the system. Since each case is evaluated by 3 participants, micro- and macro-averages will be similar.

Accuracy results: Table 4 shows the accuracy figures for the underlying methods. Mitra's and McCarthy's methods perform better for sense representation, and Mitra's method performs very well for discriminative sense detection. For discriminative sense detection, there were a few undecided cases[5]. As per overall confidence, we observe that McCarthy's method performs the best. Note that the number of candidate senses returned by McCarthy were much less in comparison to the other methods. Mitra's method performs comparably for both the time periods, while Lau's method performs comparably only for 2006-2008.

Inter-annotator agreement: The inter-annotator agreement for the three methods using Fleiss' kappa is shown in Table 6. We see that the inter-annotator agreement for Question 2 is much less in comparison to that for Question 1. This is quite natural since Question 2 is much more difficult to answer than Question 1 even for humans.

Comparison among methods: Further, we wanted to check the relative performance of the three approaches on a common set of words. McCarthy's output did not have any overlap with the other methods but for Lau and Mitra, among the

---

[5]This happens when one of the three annotators responded the first question as 'No', thus leaving only two valid responses for the second question. If both responses do not match, majority voting will remain undecided.

Table 4: Accuracy figures for the three methods from manual evaluation.

Method	Time-period	Sense Representation		Sense Discrimination			Overall Confidence	
		Majority voting	Average	Majority voting	Average	Undecided	Majority voting	Average
Lau	1987-1995	46.67%	60.0%	40.0%	61.82%	33.33%	30.0%	37.78%
	2006-2008	70.0%	67.78%	50.0%	**63.93%**	23.33%	43.33%	44.44%
McCarthy	1987-1995	**76.67%**	**77.78%**	66.67%	**78.57%**	20.0%	**56.67%**	**61.11%**
	2006-2008	66.67%	68.89%	53.33%	55.0%	6.67%	**46.67%**	**48.89%**
Mitra	1987-1995	75.0%	76.19%	**73.91%**	66.2%	**17.86%**	50.0%	50.0%
	2006-2008	**87.5%**	**80.21%**	**60.0%**	57.47%	**6.25%**	44.79%	46.88%

Table 5: Comparison of accuracy figures for 30 overlap words between Lau and Mitra.

Method	Sense Representation		Sense Discrimination			Overall Confidence	
	Majority voting	Average	Majority voting	Average	Undecided	Majority voting	Average
Lau	50.0%	53.33%	**65.38%**	**55.56%**	13.33%	26.67%	26.67%
Mitra	**90.0%**	**84.44%**	50.0%	48.89%	13.33%	**41.11%**	**43.33%**

Table 6: Fleiss' kappa for the three methods

	Lau	McCarthy	Mitra
Question 1	0.40	0.31	0.41
Question 2	0.19	0.12	0.12

words selected for manual evaluation, 30 words were common. We show the comparison results in Table 5. While Lau performs better on discriminative sense detection accuracy, Mitra performs much better overall.

6 Discussion

In this section, we discuss the results further by analyzing some of the responses. In Table 7, we provide one example entry each for all the three possible responses for the three methods.

Lau's method: In Lau's method, consider the word 'navigation'. Its news-specific sense cluster corresponds to a device to accurately ascertaining one's position and planning and following a route. The sense clusters in books corpus relate to navigation as a passage for ships among other senses and are different from the news-specific sense. The participants accordingly evaluated it as a news-specific sense. For the word 'fencing', the book-specific cluster corresponds to the sense of fencing as a sports in which participants fight with swords under some rules. We can see that the first sense cluster from news corpus has a similar sense and accordingly, it was not judged as a corpus-specific sense. Finally, the book-specific cluster of 'stalemate' does not denote any coherent sense, as also judged by the evaluators.

McCarthy's method: In McCarthy's method, consider the word 'pisces'. The book-specific cluster corresponds to the 12th sign of the zodiac in astrology. None of the clusters in the news corpus denote this sense and it was evaluated as book-specific. For the word 'filibuster', the news-specific sense corresponds to an adventurer in a private military action in a foreign country. We can see that the cluster in the other corpus has the same sense and was not judged as corpus-specific. The news-specific sense cluster for the word 'agora' does not correspond to any coherent sense of the word and was accordingly judged.

Mitra's method: Finally, coming to Mitra's method, consider the word 'chain'. Its news-specific cluster corresponds to the sense of a series of establishments, such as stores, theaters, or hotels, under a common ownership or management. The sense clusters in books corpus, on the other hand, relate to chemical bonds, series of links of metals, polymers, etc. Thus, this sense of 'chain' was evaluated as news-specific. Take the word 'divider'. Its book-specific cluster corresponds to an electrical device used for various measurements. We can see that some of the clusters in the news corpus also have a similar sense (e.g., 'pulses, amplifiers, proportional, pulse, signal, frequencies, amplifier, voltage'). Thus, this particular sense of 'divider' was not judged as a corpus-specific sense. Finally, the news-specific cluster of the word 'explanations' does not look very coherent and was judged as not representing a sense of explanations.

In general, corpus-specific senses, such as 'navigation' as 'gps, device, software' being news-specific, 'pisces' as '12th sign of the zodiac' being book-specific and 'chain' as 'series of establishment' being news-specific look quite sensible.

Table 7: Example cases from the evaluation: First column mentions the method name, which corpus-specific, time-period and the candidate word. Second column mentions the responses to the two questions. Corpus-specific sense cluster is shown in third column and fourth column shows the sense clusters in the other corpus, separated by '##'.

Description	Response	Corpus-specific sense cluster	Sense clusters in other corpus
Lau, **News**, 2006-2008, navigation	Yes, Yes	devices, gps, systems, company, mobile, portable, device, software, oriental, steam, co., peninsular, market, personal, products, ports, tomtom, car, digital, …	company, river, commerce, steam, act, system, free, mississippi, …## spend, academic, according, activities, age, area, artistic, athletic, …## engaged, devoted, literary, agricultural, intellectual, devote, interest, occupied, …## pleasures, nature, mind, literature, amusements, …
Lau, **Book**, 2006-2008, fencing	Yes, No	riding, dancing, taught, exercises, boxing, drawing, horses, archery, study, horsemanship, music, swimming, wrestling, schools, …	team, club, olympic, school, women, sport, sports, gold, …## border, miles, barriers, build, billion, congress, bill, illegal, …## security, wire, area, park, construction, fence, property, city, …
Lau, **Book**, 1987-1995, stalemate	No, NA	york, break, hansen, south, front, hill, turned, bloody, north, western, provide, knopf, talbott, breaking, …	political, government, minister, president, prime, opposition, coalition, aimed, …## budget, house, congress, federal, tax, bush, white, senate, …## war, military, ended, president, states, talks, peace, conflict, …
McCarthy, **Book**, 2006-2008, pisces	Yes , Yes	scorpio, aquarius, libra, aries, sagittarius, leo, cancer, constellation, constellations, orion, capricornus, scorpius, perseus, uranus, pluto, auriga, andromeda, bootes, ophiuchus, …	protocol, putt, shootings, aspect, golf, yes, relationships, onset, …## tablets, economist, guides, realist, officer, attorney, trustees, chairmen, …## hearings, bottom, peak, surface, floors, floor, walls, berm, …
McCarthy, **News**, 2006-2008, filibuster	Yes, No	rebellion, insurgency, combat, decision, campaign, crackdown, determination, objections, crusade, amendments, offensive, wars, interference, assault, violation, battle, dishonesty, …	pirates, raiders, invaders, adventurers, bandits, smugglers, freebooters, privateers, vikings, robbers, corsairs, outlaws, buccaneers, rebels, traders, marauders, tribesmen, brigands, slavers, insurgents, …
McCarthy, **News**, 1987-1995, agora	No, NA	opinions, restriction, appetite, rubric, pandions, authorizations, nato, delegations, bannockburn, dm, ceding, resolve, industrialization, cry, miracle, gop, shortage, navy, yes, multimedia, …	marketplace, plaza, courtyard, acropolis, stadium, precinct, sanctuary, pompeii, piazza, auditorium, temple, synagogues, basilica, synagogue, cemeteries, arena, gymnasium, palace, portico, amphitheatre, …
Mitra, **News**, 2006-2008, chain	Yes, Yes	carrier, empire, business, retailer, bank, supplier, franchise, franchises, corporation, firms, brands, distributor, firm, seller, group, organization, lender, conglomerate, provider, businesses, manufacturer, giant, company, …	fiber, filament, polymer, hydrocarbon, …## network, mesh, lattice, …## ladder, hierarchy, …## subunit, molecules, protein, macromolecules, molecule, subunits, receptor, chains, …## bracelet, necklaces, earrings, brooch, necklace, bracelets, pendant, rosary, …## pin, knot, noose, girdle, knob, scarf, leash, pulley, …## bond, bonds, …## never, still, fast, …## non, …## proton, …## test, four, per, triple, ten, multi, two, square …## air, neck, computer, under, cigar, bank, load, pressure, …
Mitra, **Book**, 1987-1995, divider	Yes, No	potentiometer, voltmeter, oscilloscope, converters, oscillator, connector, amplifier, filtering, coupler, filter, microphone, accelerator, reflector, relay, signal, probe, regulator, preamplifier, oscillators, array, multiplier, …	pulses, amplifiers, proportional, pulse, signal, frequencies, amplifier, voltage, …## chip, circuits, circuitry, clock, arrays, …## chambers, wall, junction, openings, barriers, dividers, semiconductor, wires, …## below, level, above, deviation, …## truck, planes, plane, van, motorists, lanes, …## addresses, …## along, gate, stone, gates, fence, …## modes, widths, rotation, projection, form, densities, model …
Mitra, **News**, 1987-1995, explanations	No, NA	way, qualities, phrases, indications, impression, manner, experience, wisdom, assumption, view, judgments, rumors, sentences, …	causes, evidence, …## theses, motivations, judgements, analyses, inferences, answers, definitions, predictions, …## proxy, blame, accounting, reasons, accounting, blamed, remedies, compensates, …

Table 8: Results for different thresholds of McCarthy's method to make a total of 50 words. Each cell represents the total number of words (number of candidate words chosen for a threshold + number of candidate words from the previous thresholds = total number of candidate words) (overall confidence).

		Upper Threshold		
		0.45	0.40	0.35
Lower Threshold	0.05	69 (2) (50%)	105 (2 + (2)) (50%)	152 (2 + (4)) (33.33%)
	0.10	267 (6 + (2)) (62.5%)	406 (4 + (10)) (50.0%)	615 (6 + (16)) (45.45%)
	0.15	587 (10 + (8)) (66.67%)	891 (6 + (24)) (56.67%)	1442 (12 + (38)) (54.0%)

7 Parameter Tuning

To make our experiments more rigorous, we performed parameter tuning on Lau's and McCarthy's method to find the optimal accuracy value. We decided to select 50 words from each method to evaluate. 11 words out of these are from the time period 1987–1995 and the rest from the time period 2006–2008.

Lau's method: For Lau's method, the thresholds represent maximum similarity. So, a lower value will be more restrictive as compared to a higher value. We selected three thresholds (0.30, 0.35, 0.40) for Lau's method for our experiment. Table 9 shows the total number of candidate words, words selected and average accuracy (overall confidence) of each threshold. First, we randomly selected 0.26% words from the most restrictive threshold (i.e., 0.30). For the next threshold (0.35), since it contains all the words of the lower threshold (0.30), we we randomly selected 0.26% words from the remaining 3715 words. We did the same for the threshold 0.40 again. Using the 50 words thus obtained, we performed the evaluation. We used the same evaluation method as outlined in Section 5.

McCarthy's method: For McCarthy's method, we have an upper and a lower threshold. A higher value for upper threshold and/or a lower value for lower threshold, would mean that it is more restrictive. Thus, a value of 0.45 for upper threshold and 0.05 for lower threshold would be the most restrictive in our set of thresholds. The total number of words, the number of words selected for evaluation and overall confidence are shown in Table 8. We used the same technique as we applied for Lau's method to evaluate a total of 50 words.

We can see that a higher value (less restrictive) of the threshold provides better results in case of Lau. For McCarthy, we infer that a higher value (more restrictive) of upper threshold and a higher value (less restrictive) of the lower threshold is optimal.

Table 9: Average accuracy for different threshold values in Lau's method.

Threshold	0.30	0.35	0.40
Total Words	11537	15252	19745
Words Selected	30	9 + (30)	11 + (39)
Average	16.67%	28.2%	32.0 %

8 Conclusions and future work

To summarize, we adapted three different methods for novel and predominant sense detection to identify cross corpus-specific word senses. In particular, we used multi-stage filtering to restrict the candidate senses by Mitra's method, used JS similarity across the sense clusters of two different corpora sources in Lau's method and used thresholds on the normalized prevalence score as well as the concept of denoting sense cluster using the most contributing neighbors in McCarthy's method. From the example cases, it is quite clear that after our adaptations, the outputs of the three proposed methods have very similar formats. Manual evaluation results were quite decent and in most of the cases, overall confidence in the methods was around 45-60%. There is certainly scope in future for using advanced methods for comparing sense clusters, which can improve the accuracy of discriminative sense detection by these algorithms. Further, it will also be interesting to look into novel ways of combining results from different approaches.

References

Adam Jatowt and Kevin Duh. 2014. A framework for analyzing semantic change of words across time. In *Proceedings of the Joint JCDL/TPDL Digital Libraries Conference.*

Adam Kilgarriff, Pavel Rychly, Pavel Smrz, David Tugwell. 2004. The sketch engine. In Proceedings of *EURALEX*, 105–116, Lorient, France.

Adam Kilgarriff, David Tugwell. 2001. Word sketch: Extraction and display of significant collocations for lexicography. In proceedings of *COLLOCATION: Computational Extraction, Analysis and Exploitation*, 32–38, Toulouse, France.

Andrs Kornai 1997. Zipf's law outside the middle range Proc. Sixth Meeting on *Mathematics of Language*, Florida, USA pp. 347-356.

Beate Dorow and Dominic Widdows. 2003. Discovering corpus-specific word senses. In *Proceedings of the Tenth Conference on European Chapter of the Association for Computational Linguistics - Volume 2*, EACL '03, pages 79–82, Stroudsburg, PA, USA. Association for Computational Linguistics.

Chris Biemann. 2006. Chinese whispers - an efficient graph clustering algorithm and its application to natural language processing problems. In proceedings of *TextGraphs*, 73–80, New York City, NY, USA.

Chris Biemann. 2011. *Structure Discovery in Natural Language*. Springer Heidelberg Dordrecht London New York. ISBN 978-3-642-25922-7.

Chris Biemann and Martin Riedl. 2013. Text: Now in 2D! A Framework for Lexical Expansion with Contextual Similarity. *Journal of Language Modelling*, 1(1), 55–95.

Christiane Fellbaum (ed.) 1998. WordNet: An Electronic Lexical Database Cambridge, MA: MIT Press

David M. Blei and Andrew Y. Ng and Michael I. Jordan and John Lafferty. 2003. Latent dirichlet allocation. *Journal of Machine Learning Research*, pages 993-1022.

David M. Blei and John D. Lafferty. 2006. Dynamic topic models. In proceedings of *ICML*, 113–120, Pittsburgh, Pennsylvania.

Diana Mccarthy and Rob Koeling and Julie Weeds and John Carroll. 2004. Finding Predominant Word Senses in Untagged Text. In *Proceedings of the 42nd Annual Meeting of the Association for Computational Linguistics*, pages 280–287.

Hinrich Schütze. 1998. Automatic word sense discrimination. *Computational Linguistics*, 24(1):97–123.

Jey Han Lau, Paul Cook, Diana McCarthy, David Newman, and Timothy Baldwin. 2012. Word sense induction for novel sense detection. In *Proceedings of the 13th Conference of the European Chapter of the Association for Computational Linguistics*, EACL '12, pages 591–601.

Jey Han Lau, Paul Cook, Diana McCarthy, Spandana Gella and Timothy Baldwin 2014. Learning Word Sense Distributions, Detecting Unattested Senses and Identifying Novel Senses Using Topic Models. In *Proceedings of the 52nd Annual Meeting of the Association for Computational Linguistics (ACL 2014)*, Baltimore, USA.

Karen Spärk-Jones. 1986. *Synonymy and Semantic Classification*. Edinburgh University Press. ISBN 0-85224-517-3.

Katrin Erk, Diana Mccarthy, Nicholas Gaylord. 2010. Investigations on word senses and word usages In proceedings of *ACL*, Suntec, Singapore

Kristina Gulordava, Marco Baroni. 2011. A distributional similarity approach to the detection of semantic change in the Google Books Ngram corpus. In proceedings of the workshop on *Geometrical Models for Natural Language Semantics*, EMNLP 2011.

Lea Frermann and Mirella Lapata 2016. A Bayesian Model of Diachronic Meaning Change. *Transactions of the Association for Computational Linguistics 2016* , vol 4, (pp. 31-45)

Nancy Ide, Jean Vronis. 1998. Introduction to the special issue on word sense disambiguation: The state of the art. *Computational Linguistics*, 24(1):1–40.

Nina Tahmasebi, Thomas Risse, Stefan Dietze. 2011. Towards automatic language evolution tracking: a study on word sense tracking. In proceedings of *EvoDyn*, vol. 784, Bonn, Germany.

Patrick Pantel and Dekang Lin. 2002. Discovering word senses from text *Proceedings of the eighth ACM SIGKDD international conference on Knowledge discovery and data mining*, pp 613-619, ACM.

Paul Cook, Jey Han Lau, Michael Rundell, Diana Mccarthy, Timothy Baldwin 2013. A lexicographic appraisal of an automatic approach for detecting new word senses. In proceedings of *eLex*, 49-65, Tallinn, Estonia.

Paul Cook, Suzanne Stevenson. 2010. Automatically Identifying Changes in the Semantic Orientation of Words. In proceedings of *LREC*, Valletta, Malta

Pavel Rychlý and Adam Kilgarriff. 2007. An efficient algorithm for building a distributional thesaurus (and other sketch engine developments). In proceedings of *ACL, poster and demo sessions*, 41–44, Prague, Czech Republic.

Pelevina Maria, Nikolay Arefyev, Chris Biemann, and Alexander Panchenko. 2016. Making sense of word embeddings. *In Proceedings of the 1st Workshop on Representation Learning for NLP*, pp. 174-183. Berlin, Germany

Roberto Navigli. 2009. Word sense disambiguation: a survey. *ACM Computing Surveys*, 41(2):1–69.

Samuel Brody and Mirella Lapata. 2009. Bayesian word sense induction. In *Proceedings of the 12th Conference of the European Chapter of the Association for Computational Linguistics*, EACL '09, pages 103–111, Stroudsburg, PA, USA. Association for Computational Linguistics.

Shanta Phani, Shibamouli Lahiri, and Arindam Biswas. 2012. Culturomics on a bengali newspaper corpus. In *Proceedings of the 2012 International Conference on Asian Language Processing*, IALP '12, pages 237–240, Washington, DC, USA. IEEE Computer Society.

Sunny Mitra, Ritwik Mitra, Martin Riedl, Chris Biemann, Animesh Mukherjee and Pawan Goyal. 2014. That's sick dude!: Automatic identification of word sense change across different timescales. In proceedings of *ACL*, 1020–1029, Baltimore, USA.

Sunny Mitra, Ritwik Mitra, Suman Kalyan Maity, Martin Riedl, Chris Biemann, Pawan Goyal and Animesh Mukherjee. 2015. An automatic approach to identify word sense changes in text media across timescales. *JNLE Special issue on 'Graph methods for NLP'* (forthcoming).

Vivek Kulkarni, Rami Al-Rfou, Bryan Perozzi, and Steven Skiena. 2015. Statistically significant detection of linguistic change. *CoRR*, abs/1411.3315.

Xuchen Yao and Benjamin Van Durme. 2011. Nonparametric bayesian word sense induction. In *Proceedings of TextGraphs-6: Graph-based Methods for Natural Language Processing*, TextGraphs-6, pages 10–14, Stroudsburg, PA, USA.

Xuerui Wang, Andrew Mccallum. 2006. Topics over time: a non-Markov continuous-time model of topical trends. In proceedings of *KDD*, 424–433, Philadelphia, PA, USA.

Yee Whye Teh and Michael I. Jordan and Matthew J. Beal and David M. Blei 2006. Hierarchical dirichlet processes. *Journal of the American statistical association*, 101(476).

Yoav Goldberg, Jon Orwant. 2013. A dataset of syntactic-ngrams over time from a very large corpus of English books. In proceedings of the *Joint Conference on Lexical and Computational Semantics (*SEM)*, 241–247, Atlanta, GA, USA.

Merging knowledge bases in different languages

Jerónimo Hernández-González
University of the Basque
Country, Donostia, GI, Spain
`jeronimo.hernandez@ehu.eus`

Estevam R. Hruschka Jr.
Federal University of Sao
Carlos, São Carlos, SP, Brazil
`estevam@dc.ufscar.br`

Tom M. Mitchell
Carnegie Mellon University,
Pittsburgh, PA, USA
`tom.mitchell@cs.cmu.edu`

Abstract

Recently, different systems which learn to populate and extend a knowledge base (KB) from the web in different languages have been presented. Although a large set of concepts should be learnt independently from the language used to read, there are facts which are expected to be more easily gathered in local language (e.g., culture or geography). A system that merges KBs learnt in different languages will benefit from the complementary information as long as common beliefs are identified, as well as from redundancy present in web pages written in different languages. In this paper, we deal with the problem of identifying equivalent beliefs (or concepts) across language specific KBs, assuming that they share the same ontology of categories and relations. In a case study with two KBs independently learnt from different inputs, namely web pages written in English and web pages written in Portuguese respectively, we report on the results of two methodologies: an approach based on personalized PageRank and an inference technique to find out common relevant paths through the KBs. The proposed inference technique efficiently identifies relevant paths, outperforming the baseline (a dictionary-based classifier) in the vast majority of tested categories.

1 Introduction

In the last few decades, the machine learning community has launched different research projects to take advantage of the massive source of information which has become the web, and of the people who build it up. Among others, information extraction systems (IES) which use the text found in webpages to extract, validate and incorporate beliefs to a structured knowledge base have been developed (e.g., YAGO (Suchanek et al., 2008), NELL (Mitchell et al., 2015) or Knowledge Vault (Dong et al., 2014)). Such knowledge bases (KBs) store facts about the real world, which are represented as entities and relationship among entities. The reliability of a fact, inferred from the web, is at first questionable due to the *noisy* information available on the Web. This difficulty is usually overcome by relying on data redundancy from multiple Web pages. Requiring higher degrees of redundancy to incorporate beliefs to the KB help to improve the quality of the learnt KB.

In the long run, having two such IES, running independently, tend to generate equivalent KBs, even if they gather information from different webpages, in different time or using different terminology. However, if those two systems extract (and store) facts from Web pages written in different languages, it can be hard to automatically identify redundant facts, or to automatically merge such KBs. Let us assume an English KB containing the concept of the city of *Sao Carlos* as a belief and, also, a Portuguese KB with the equivalent concept represented in Portuguese as *São Carlos*. Let us assume also that, in the Portuguese KB, *São Carlos* is linked to the concept *Paulo Altomani*, the major of the city. Combining both KBs and identifying the equivalence between *Sao Carlos* (en) and *São Carlos* (pt) can help to automatically populate the English KB adding the fact that *Paulo Altomani* is the mayor of *Sao Carlos* (en).

In this paper we deal with the problem of merging KBs learnt in different languages. This task consists of ontology alignment and equivalent concept matching. We use graph-based inference techniques to deal with the problem of identifying

Proceedings of TextGraphs-11: the Workshop on Graph-based Methods for Natural Language Processing, ACL 2017, pages 21–29,
Vancouver, Canada, August 3, 2017. ©2017 Association for Computational Linguistics

equivalent entities in different KBs assuming that, in spite of being learnt independently, they share a common ontology. The contributions of this work are as follows:

- An approach to multi-lingual KB merging based on Personalized PageRank

- A path-based graph inference approach that shows promising results when compared to Personalized PageRank.

- An empirical analysis by means of a case study. When graph connectivity is enhanced by means of a SVO corpus, results stand out.

In the remainder of this paper we first provide a formal description of the problem, which is formulated as an inference problem. Then, the proposed solutions are presented. In Section 4, the different approaches are tested in a case study with two KBs independently learnt by NELL (Mitchell et al., 2015) from English and Portuguese web-pages respectively. Next, their behavior is discussed. The paper finishes with conclusions and ideas for future work.

2 Framework

Consider a Knowledge Base (KB) K as a tuple (O, I_c, I_r, S). The ontology O is represented by a 4-tuple (C, H_C, R, H_R), where H_C codifies the hierarchy among categories $c \in C$ (e.g., the category *city* is a specification of the category *place*) and, similarly, H_R codifies the hierarchy among relation-types $r(c_1, c_2) \in R$ with $c_1, c_2 \in C$ (e.g., *locatedAt(city, country)* is more general than *capitalOf(city, country)*). I_c and I_r are the sets of entities and relationships, respectively, that populate the KB. Thus, an instance $(e, c) \in I_c$ assigns entity e to category $c \in C$ (e.g., *(Pittsburgh, city)* or *(USA, country)*) and each instance $(e_1, r, e_2) \in I_r$ is a relation of type r which associates two entities, e_1 and e_2, with $(e_1, c_1) \in I_c$, $(e_2, c_2) \in I_c$ and $r(c_1, c_2) \in R$ (e.g., *(Pittsburgh, locatedAt, USA)*). S involves the literal strings which are used to refer to the entities. Two —or more— literal strings s_1 and s_2 ($s_1 \neq s_2$) can refer to the same entity e $((s_1, e) \in S \wedge (s_2, e) \in S)$, and the same literal string s can refer to two different entities e_1 and e_2 as well $((s, e_1) \in S \wedge (s, e_2) \in S$ with $e_1 \neq e_2)$. For example, the literal strings "Steal City" and "Pittsburgh" can refer to the concept *Pittsburgh*, whereas "New York" could refer to both *NYC* and *New York State*.

Graph representation. In this paper, a graph representation of the KB is used and the problem of merging KBs in different languages is handled as a graph inference problem. Each entity e is represented as a node. Each relation instance $(e_1, r, e_2) \in I_r$ is represented by an edge of type r between the nodes representing entities e_1 and e_2. Similarly, for each $(s, e) \in S$, string s is represented as a node and an edge of type *canReferTo* links it to entity e. In the remaining of the paper, the terms "nodes" and "entities", on the one hand, and "relation" and "edge types", on the other, are interchangeably used.

2.1 Inferring entity-equivalence across KBs in different languages

For the sake of simplicity, let us follow the example of our case study to describe the problem of merging two KBs which share the same ontology structure (categories and relation types) but which have been learnt (populated) in different languages. Given both KBs, $K^{en} = (O, I_c^{en}, I_r^{en})$ and $K^{pt} = (O, I_c^{pt}, I_r^{pt})$, in English and Portuguese respectively, the merging process $K^* = merge(K^{en}, K^{pt})$ consists mainly of the union of both sets of entities $I_c^* = I_c^{pt} \cup I_c^{en}$, where only an instance of the equivalent entities across languages (e.g., *New York* or *Nova Iorque*) remains. As a consequence of this first step, the sets of relation instances $I_r^* = I_r^{pt} \cup I_r^{en}$ is similarly merged: two relation instances in different languages, (e_1^{en}, r, e_2^{en}) and (e_1^{pt}, r, e_2^{pt}), are equivalent if their relation type $r \in R$ is the same and the associated entities are fused in I_c^* ($e_1^{en} \sim e_1^{pt}$ and $e_2^{en} \sim e_2^{pt}$). To avoid losing information, per-language literal string sets (S^{en}, S^{pt}) are kept linked to the corresponding entities in I_c^*.

The key step is, therefore, the identification of equivalent entities across languages. Let us introduce the relation types $(e^{en}, equivalentTo, e^{pt})$, which connects two entities in different language specific KBs, and $(s^{en}, canBeTranslatedAs, s^{pt})$, which relates two literal strings which are the translation of each other in the different languages. Thus, the originally independent language specific KBs become connected and the problem of finding equivalent entities across languages can be reformulated as inferring the existence of *equivalentTo* relationships (edges) between pairs of entities (nodes) in different KBs (subgraphs).

3 Methods

In this study, we make use of inference techniques over graphs to find equivalent entities in different language KBs: a Personalized PageRank (PPR) (Haveliwala, 2002) based approach and another one based on Path Ranking Algorithm (PRA) (Lao and Cohen, 2010). Both techniques produce classification models which, given a new pair of entities, predict whether or not an *equivalentTo* relationship is suitable among them.

3.1 Personalized PageRank based approach

In the context of webpage ranking, Personalized PageRank (Haveliwala, 2002) was designed to bias the result of the original PageRank algorithm (Page et al., 1999) to make it topic-sensitive. It can be seen as a similarity measure that characterizes the neighborhood of a node X in a graph. Formally, it estimates a probability distribution over the nodes of the graph. Considering X as the source node of a random walk, it estimates the probability of reaching node Y after w random steps. At time t, the next step follows one of the out-edges of current node X_t with equal probability $(1 - \alpha) \cdot \frac{1}{|X_t|}$ (where $|X_t|$ is the out-degree of node X_t) or jumps back to the source node X with probability α. The stationary probability distribution is usually approximated by sampling a number n of random walks with probability α of restarting at source node X. The probability assigned to node Y is the proportion of walks which finish at Y.

In the context of this work, PPR has been used to measure similarity between nodes. Assuming that two equivalent entities in different language subgraphs (L_1 and L_2) will be highly connected through a number of different paths, the equivalent entity $e_t^{L_2}$ is expected to be assigned a high probability by a PPR with origin at entity $e_o^{L_1}$. Using PPR to estimate the probability distribution $p(\cdot|e_o^{L_1})$, a classification model is built by imposing three conditions: (1) the predicted equivalent entity belongs to a different language subgraph ($e_t^{L_2} : L_1 \neq L_2$), (2) the category of both the source and target entities is the same or compatible (both are in the same hierarchical line in H_C):

$$(e_o^{L_1}, c_o) \in I_c^{L_1} \wedge (e_t^{L_2}, c_t) \in I_c^{L_2} :$$

$$c_o, c_t \in C \wedge (c_o = c_t \vee c_o \stackrel{H_C}{\rightleftharpoons} c_t)$$

and (3) the probability of the predicted entity exceeds threshold $h \leq p(e_t^{L_2}|e_o^{L_1})$.

3.2 Path Ranking algorithm based approach

The Path Ranking algorithm (Lao and Cohen, 2010) transforms the task of inferring new relationships of type r between pairs of entities into a binary classification problem: given a new pair of nodes, is a relationship of type r suitable between them? To do so, it generates, in two steps, a training matrix from which any type of classifier can be learnt. The pairs of nodes already connected by a relationship of type r are positive pairs or examples in this approach. During the first step, paths (sequence of relation types, $r_1, r_2, \ldots, r_p$) commonly connecting the nodes of the positive pairs are identified by running a number of random walks of limited length. In the second step, a training matrix is built such that each identified path constitutes a feature (column) and each pair is a positive example (row). Each cell (i, j) of the matrix is assigned the probability of reaching the target node e_t^i of the i-th pair using a random walk that follows the sequence of relation types of the j-th path with origin at node e_o^i.

Departing from the original design, the generation of paths has been adapted to take advantage of the particularities of our application. First of all, note that every path which connects two nodes in different language subgraphs, e^{en} and e^{pt}, includes an *equivalentTo* or *canBeTranslatedAs* relation type. Note also that, assuming a common ontology for both KBs, the relation types and categories are the same in both languages. The idea behind the original PRA —i.e., certain relationships (or paths) can be particularly relevant for determining the equivalence of entities of a specific category— is extended to the multi-language context by looking for relevant paths which appear replicated in both language subgraphs. Suppose that there is a *Di Blassio* entity in both languages and an *equivalentTo* relationship links them. Suppose also that there are (*Di Blassio, isMayorOf, New York City*) and (*Di Blassio, isPrefeitoDe, Cidade de Nova Iorque*) relationships in English and Portuguese subgraphs respectively. Knowing that (*New York City, Cidade de Nova Iorque*) are equivalent, *isMayorOf* can be considered as a relevant path (of length one) to predict the equivalence of *cities*. Intuitively, a person cannot be mayor of different cities.

Our search for relevant paths starts, for each positive pair, with a breadth-first search from the source node $e_o^{L_1}$ looking for nodes $e_b^{L_1}$ with an across-language edge (edge type *equivalentTo* or *canBeTranslatedAs*). For each of these nodes, the node $e_b^{L_2}$ at the other extreme of the across-language relationship is taken. Then, the path followed to reach $e_b^{L_1}$ from $e_o^{L_1}$ is reversed. If the reversed path connects $e_b^{L_2}$ to the target node $e_t^{L_2}$ of the corresponding positive pair, the whole path from $e_o^{L_1}$ to $e_t^{L_2}$ is kept for evaluation. The relevance of a path $(r_1, r_2, \ldots, r_p)$ is measured as the probability of reaching the target node following a random walk (through relationships of types $r_1, r_2, \ldots$) starting at source node, or in the opposite direction. Thus, the most relevant path always leads to the opposite node of the pair, and only to it. Uninformative paths, those whose rates are below the average, are filtered out. With the remaining relevant paths, a training matrix is built in the same way as the original PRA.

4 Experiments

A complete set of experiments has been designed to test the performance of both approaches in the task of identifying equivalent concepts across languages. A baseline based on dictionary translations is used to put these results in context.

4.1 Knowledge bases

The knowledge bases used in these experiments correspond to the 970th and 110th iterations of the English and Portuguese versions of NELL, respectively. As aforementioned, a graph is obtained from each KB drawing a node for each entity and literal string and a labeled edge for each relationship among entities. Moreover, edges of type *canReferTo* link each entity with its literal strings. We found out that many entities in both KBs are isolated, i.e., they have no relationship. For these experiments, all the isolated nodes have been pruned from the graphs as our techniques cannot deal with them: both presented techniques make use of the relationships among entities to perform. The resulting graph is used below in a first set of experiments.

As previously mentioned, both PPR and PRA-based techniques make use of relationships and, in fact, they need well connected graphs to perform correctly. However, the graphs obtained from NELL KBs are quite sparse (see Table 1 for

	English	
Category	GRAPH 1	GRAPH 2
animal	13.32 ± 47.12	392.02 ± 1859.43
country	22.65 ± 68.60	289.97 ± 970.55
city	5.00 ± 22.31	134.72 ± 1176.05
movie	1.60 ± 1.69	88.95 ± 891.37
person	2.99 ± 6.76	244.10 ± 1394.07
writer	2.72 ± 4.75	43.50 ± 419.41
actor	2.19 ± 2.12	77.21 ± 819.10
sport	19.94 ± 132.71	256.49 ± 1430.06
all	4.48 ± 28.95	275.49 ± 1715.53

	Portuguese	
Category	GRAPH 1	GRAPH 2
animal	1.57 ± 1.17	27.23 ± 58.58
pais	5.04 ± 15.99	180.79 ± 820.71
cidade	1.71 ± 4.33	32.03 ± 135.13
filme	1.33 ± 0.79	34.77 ± 177.64
pessoa	1.18 ± 0.66	16.62 ± 101.67
escritor	1.15 ± 0.46	6.40 ± 12.04
ator	1.67 ± 1.41	6.96 ± 11.40
esporte	3.88 ± 6.31	26.98 ± 83.30
all	1.81 ± 3.93	51.26 ± 199.03

Table 1: For each language and category, mean out-degree value and associated standard deviation of the nodes of that category in the (first) graph, without isolated nodes, and in the (second) graph, fed with SVO-inferred relationships before pruning. The last row sums up all the categories.

its mean out-degree). An enhanced connectivity among entities is achieved considering a SVO corpus. A SVO consists of statistics about the presence of a triplet *subject-verb-object* in a text corpus usually crawled from the Web. In this study, Wijaya and Mitchell (2016) method to map verbs found in a corpus to relationships of a given structured KB has been used. It explores a SVO corpus looking for verbs which can be used to represent the different relation types $r \in R$ of an ontology O. Given the returned set of representative verbs for a specific relation type r, pairs of literal strings $s_1, s_2 \in S$ which appear linked by means of one or more representative verbs in the SVO corpus can be considered as evidence of a r relationship. In practice, all the entities which can be referred to by s_1 and s_2 are connected by means of an edge of type r. As can be observed in Table 1, connectivity is largely enhanced. On average, the number of edges connecting each node has increased although, according to the related standard deviations, the behavior is not uniform. The graph resulting from this enhancing process is used in a second set of experiments.

Note that the enhancement with SVO-inferred

English			
Category	UNPROCESSED	GRAPH 1	GRAPH 2
animal	12,436 (36)	591 (23)	746 (27)
country	6,031 (106)	443 (93)	460 (93)
city	18,893 (460)	4,437 (237)	5,311 (263)
movie	7,008 (42)	712 (38)	831 (38)
person	6,693 (403)	2,898 (395)	3,050 (399)
writer	18,911 (61)	1,707 (39)	2,143 (40)
actor	28,361 (512)	794 (139)	1,421 (167)
sport	5,022 (109)	205 (66)	381 (75)
all	1,909,339 (4,126)	66,239 (2,112)	96,086 (2,331)

Portuguese			
Category	UNPROCESSED	GRAPH 1	GRAPH 2
animal	101 (36)	63 (14)	97 (35)
pais	153 (106)	94 (87)	136 (103)
cidade	5,767 (460)	483 (138)	1,404 (282)
filme	368 (42)	64 (25)	132 (40)
pessoa	621 (403)	611 (304)	614 (376)
escritor	114 (61)	26 (23)	63 (37)
ator	1,870 (512)	129 (36)	793 (208)
esporte	153 (109)	34 (29)	125 (94)
all	30,401 (4,126)	5,119 (1,827)	12,930 (2,565)

Table 2: For each language subgraph and category, the number of entities and, from these, the number of entities contained in a positive pair are shown. The three columns show counts, from left to right, for (1) the unprocessed graph, (2) the first graph, without isolated nodes, and (3) the second graph, fed with SVO-inferred relationships before pruning. The last row sums up all the categories.

relationships reduces the number of isolated nodes and, therefore, the number of pruned entities decreases. Table 2 reflects the effect of this enhancement, in terms of the number of remaining entities, on the pruning process. In the case of English, the second graph (with SVO-inferred relationships) is almost a 50% larger than the first graph. The Portuguese subgraph, in turn, grows 2.5 times.

4.2 Bridges among both language-specific KBs

Two different strategies have been carried out in this study to generate an initial set of *equivalentTo* relationships. On the one hand, a costly manual introduction of equivalence relationships was carried out. This procedure, although costly, provides highly reliable instances of the relationship. Around 400 fully reliable relationships were thus generated. On the other hand, entities which have the same name (simple matching), in spite of having been learnt in different languages, and belong to compatible categories have been considered as equivalent pairs. Both conditions are fulfilled by

up to 4,000 pairs of entities, among which *equivalentTo* edges have been added. Although the evidence may be strong, this automatically generated set of *equivalentTo* edges could involve misleading information. For example, using this approach a hypothetical entity referring to the renowned machine learning researcher (*Michael Jordan, pessoa*) in Portuguese could be connected to the former basketball player (*Michael Jordan, athlete*) in English. The pruning process explained above affects these entities too, as shown in Table 2.

Connectivity among language subgraphs at the level of literal strings (relation type *canBeTranslatedAs*) is achieved by means of a dictionary. A list of string translations has been generated combining terms found in WordNet (de Paiva and Rademaker, 2012; Fellbaum, 1998) and translations on demand making use of the Google Translate API [1]. In total, 1.4 million string translations have been obtained. These translations are used to connect nodes representing literal strings in both language subgraphs by means of edges of type *canBeTranslatedAs*.

4.3 Training examples

Standard supervised classification takes advantage of a fully labeled dataset with examples of all the classes. They are necessary to train the classification models as well as to evaluate them. The classification task at hand is a weakly supervised classification problem (Hernández-González et al., 2016); specifically, a positive-unlabeled classification problem (Calvo et al., 2007) where only positive examples are available for training: the pairs of entities related by a *equivalentTo* relationship. No negative example, understood as a pair of nodes in different language subgraphs which are not suitable to hold an *equivalentTo* relationship, is available.

However, in this context, safe procedures for generating negative examples can be figured out. Figure 1 graphically describes the procedure followed in this study, which is based on the assumption that an entity has only one equivalent entity in the opposite language KB. Thus, the source node of a positive pair *is not equivalent* to any node in the opposite subgraph different from the corresponding target node. Formally, each $(e_o^{L1}, equivalentTo, e_t^{L2})$ relationship already present in the KB is individually consid-

[1] https://cloud.google.com/translate/

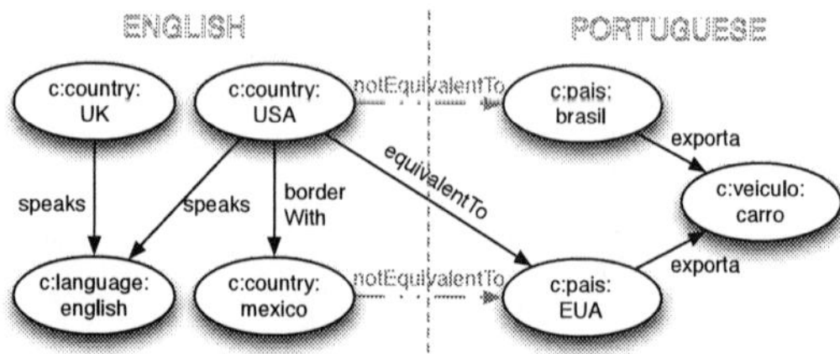

Figure 1: Generation of negative examples: given a positive pair, (*USA*, *EUA*), a walk is launched until an entity with the same category is reached: e.g., (*Mexico,Country*) by (*USA, borderWith, Mexico*). Obtained negative example: (*Mexico, EUA*).

ered. For entity $e_t^{L_2}$, other entities $e_{t'}^{L_2}$ with the same or a compatible category are identified in the same language subgraph L_2. A negative example $(e_o^{L_1}, notEquivalentTo, e_{t'}^{L_2})$ is then built using the original entity $e_o^{L_1}$ and any compatible neighbor $e_{t'}^{L_2}$. For instance, as displayed in Fig. 1, knowing that *USA* is equivalent to the Portuguese *EUA*, *Mexico* is reached from node *USA* through their common relationship (*borderWith*), thus generating a negative example (*Mexico, notEquivalentTo, EUA*). The same procedure can be carried out in the opposite direction: fixing $e_t^{L_2}$ and looking for compatible entities $e_{o'}^{L_1}$ in the neighborhood of $e_o^{L_1}$. For each positive pair, up to 2 negative pairs among all the negative examples generated in both directions are randomly selected.

4.4 Experimental settings

In addition to both described techniques, a classifier exclusively based on a dictionary is also considered. It predicts an equivalence if the nodes of the query pair represent entities with literal strings which are the translation of each other. Given that a dictionary is probably the simplest solution to deal with this problem, it has been used in this paper as a baseline.

The PPR method has been configured for these experiments with 2,000 random walks of length 5 to estimate the probability distribution, using a probability of restart equal to 0.01. Regarding our PRA-based technique, the breadth-first search is carried out to a depth of 2. These values have been selected within a 20×5-fold cross validation. PPR and the baseline do not need a training step and the results are calculated over the whole training set. For each category, PRA learns a logistic regression classifier (its implementation in Weka (Frank et al., 2016)), which is evaluated in a 10×5-fold cross validation. Remember that positive pairs are *equivalentTo* relationships, which are also represented in the graph. The edges of the graph corresponding to training examples are removed for training and testing.

The PPR and PRA-based approaches, together with the baseline, have been applied over graphs 1 and 2 (without and with SVO-inferred relationships, respectively). As our PRA-based approach learns a classifier per category, a diverse set of eight categories has been selected to test the proposals and report their performance: *animal, country, city, movie, person, writer, actor* and *sport*. In Figure 2, precision-recall (PR) curves are used to describe the results in the first graph. Each subfigure displays the results for one of the selected categories. Following the same layout, Figure 3 shows the results in the second graph. Note that results in figures 2 and 3 are not directly comparable as they have been obtained from training sets of different sizes (see in Table 2 the number of positive entities remaining after pruning in graphs 1 and 2).

5 Discussion

The performance of the different techniques has been assessed for eight categories using two graphs of different sparsity. Results show the competitiveness of the solution based exclusively on a dictionary as well as the outstanding performance of our PRA-based proposal. As expected for an inference technique that intensively explores the graph looking for relevant paths, the use of the more dense SVO+pruned graph enhances the performance of the PRA-based proposal. The behavior of PPR is less regular and changes considerably among categories.

The dictionary connects, across languages, literal strings, which can be used to refer to different entities. This may affect the precision of the dictionary approach: more than one node may be reached following the across-language path *canReferTo+canBeTranslatedAs+canReferTo* from a single source node. To alleviate this effect, our implementation only predicts a positive equivalence if both nodes of a query pair have the same category. As observed in figures 2 and 3, this baseline reaches precision values equal to 1 for all the categories with the exception of *country* and *person*. Moreover, the size of the dictionary determines the

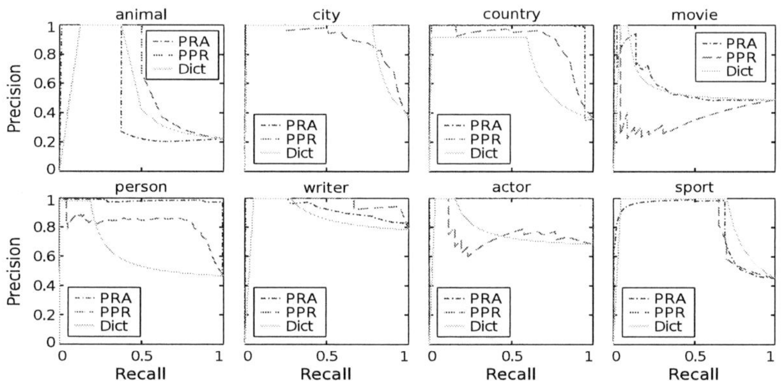

Figure 2: PR curves comparing both proposals with the dictionary as a baseline. Each figure displays the results of the three approaches with the examples of a specific category using the first graph.

maximum recall that this classifier can show before a sharp drop in precision. Thus, this approach is very competitive in categories where our dictionary translates many of the pairs (e.g., *sport*), its performance is limited in categories where few pairs are translated (e.g., *movie*).

The results of the PPR approach are difficult to interpret; no clear pattern is observed. The incorporation of new relationships from the SVO corpus does not enhance its results. Quite the opposite, it seems to harm the results in categories such as *country* or *writer*. This incorporation increases the number of edges among entities of the same language subgraph (see Table 1), while the across language connections remain the same. Intuitively, the probability of a random walk moving across language subgraphs decreases. And this crossing movement is indispensable for the PPR approach to succeed. In categories such as *animal* or *sport*, the behavior of the PPR approach matches that of the dictionary. The short path *canReferTo+canBeTranslatedAs+canReferTo* usually has few instantiations, easily leading from source to target node. Only in a few categories is the PPR approach able to overcome the baseline and, in these cases, the PRA-based approach usually outperforms it. Our PRA-based technique also imitates the dictionary approach. Intuitively, the translation path is usually considered as relevant by this technique. However, even a more complete dictionary would still lack precision in certain cases. According to its unquestionable enhanced performance, our PRA-based technique solves this problem probably relying on both the dictionary and other relevant paths. Specifically, it

is able to overcome the baseline when the dictionary is not completely precise (categories *country* and *person*). Finally, only the PRA-based technique clearly improves with the new SVO-inferred edges (categories *animal*, *writer* and *movie*).

A strategy for generating the initial *equivalentTo* relationships (Section 4.2) is the simple matching of entity names in the different languages. This already covers 403 out of 621 entities of category *person* in Portuguese. This rate is lower in category *writer*, although the same behavior would be expected since in both categories proper nouns, which are rarely translated, are used to name entities. There are two possibilities for the remaining entities: they are represented in English with a different name or they do not overlap. We carried out a manual inspection of these entities (219 in the case of *person*) to gain insight, revealing that the majority of them have Portuguese names, and those with English names do not appear in the English KB. Only a few cases have been found where a possible equivalence is present in the KBs with a slightly different name (e.g., *Max Nicholson* in English and *Dr. Max Nicholson* in Portuguese). This observation supports the idea that entities in this kind of categories, which use proper nouns, are usually complementary if an equivalence with exactly the same name is not found. In this context, the recall of the simple matching approach is expected to stand out. Our PRA-based solution would still be competitive in these categories assessing equivalences for entities with slightly different names.

The lower the number of training positive pairs for a category (Tab. 2), the worse the results of

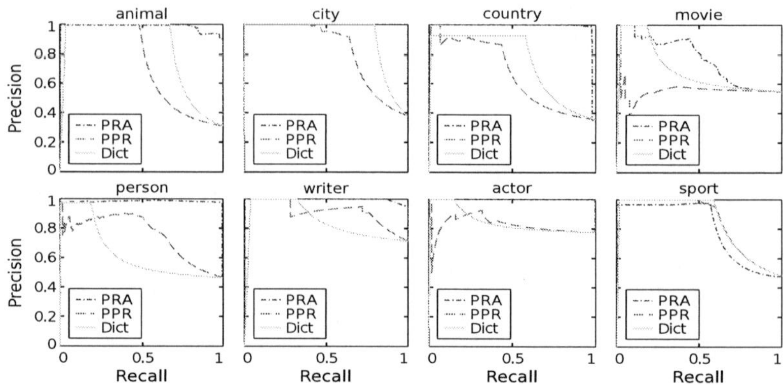

Figure 3: PR curves comparing both proposals with the dictionary as a baseline. Each figure displays the results of the three approaches with the examples of a specific category using the (second) graph pruned after populating it with new relationships inferred from a SVO corpus.

the PRA-based technique (see results for *animal, movie, writer* and *sport*). The inclusion of the relationships derived from the SVO corpus involves a considerably larger number of positive pairs in all the categories. The performance gain is noteworthy in three of them: *animal, movie* and *writer*. However, a larger number of examples does not explain the enhanced performance shown by the PRA-based approach, for example, in the *animal* category. A more densely connected graph is expected to benefit our PRA-based approach, although a larger set of edges does not directly imply a better performance. For example, despite the fact that the category *sport* shows one of the largest out-degree averages (see Tab. 1), the PRA-based classifier can neither overcome the baseline nor the PPR approach (even using the SVO-enlarged graph). Not only does the PRA-based approach require a large number of relationships, it also requires relevant paths. However, it is more likely to find a relevant path in densely connected graphs, such as that obtained after the massive incorporation of relationships from the SVO corpus. That explains the enhanced performance of our PRA-based method in categories *writer, animal* and *movie* regarding the results in the first graph without SVO-inferred relationships.

It can be agreed that the larger the number of merged KBs, the more the information which such a multi-lingual system can take advantage of. The approaches proposed in this study are designed to deal with two language subgraphs. However, applying the proposed methodology by means of pairwise comparisons, along with the

transitive property, a larger set of equivalent entities will probably be found. For example, if *New York City* is equivalent to *Cidade de Nova Iorque* (pt) and *Cidade de Nova Iorque* (pt) is equivalent to *Ciudad de Nueva York* (es), *New York City* is equivalent to *Ciudad de Nueva York* (es). Whenever the KBs learnt in the different languages are diverse enough —although partial intersection is necessary—, the probability of finding this type of triangulations rises with the number of KBs.

6 Conclusions

In this paper, we deal with the problem of merging two knowledge bases learnt from text written in different languages. Two strategies have been designed and compared with a baseline exclusively based on a dictionary. The proposed solution based on the path ranking algorithm outperforms the baseline and a second proposal based on personalized PageRank.

The PRA-based approach efficiently finds relevant paths between positive pairs of entities. The relevance of a path between two nodes is measured according to the number of entities reached following the path, in both directions. According to the experimental results, it identifies relevant paths in the majority of tested categories, specifically when a more densely connected graph is used.

For future work, taking the KB merging process as a chance for improvement, an approach to co-reference resolution could be to identify entities which have two or more equivalent entities in the opposite language subgraph. The categories of two equivalent entities could also be reassessed if these are not coincident. If this proposal is integrated into the iterative learning process of NELL, it will benefit from new entities and relationships at each new iteration, possibly leading to the discovery of new relevant paths. Before, as NELL currently allows its ontology to evolve, these proposals should be adapted to deal with unaligned ontologies, similar to what Delli Bovi et al. (2015) or Dutta et al. (2014) do.

Acknowledgments

This work was partially supported by the Basque Government, the Spanish Ministry of Economy and Competitiveness and the University of the Basque Country (IT609-13, Elkartek BID3A, TIN2016-78365-R, University-Society Project 15/19).

References

Borja Calvo, Pedro Larrañaga, and Jose A. Lozano. 2007. Learning Bayesian classifiers from positive and unlabeled examples. *Pattern Recognit. Lett.* 28(16):2375–2384.

Valeria de Paiva and Alexandre Rademaker. 2012. Revisiting a Brazilian WordNet. In *Proc. 6th Global WordNet Conf. (GWC)*. Matsue.

Claudio Delli Bovi, Luis Espinosa-Anke, and Roberto Navigli. 2015. Knowledge base unification via sense embeddings and disambiguation. In *Conf. on Empirical Methods in Natural Language*. ACL, pages 726–736.

Xin Dong, Evgeniy Gabrilovich, Geremy Heitz, Wilko Horn, Ni Lao, Kevin Murphy, Thomas Strohmann, Shaohua Sun, and Wei Zhang. 2014. Knowledge vault: A web-scale approach to probabilistic knowledge fusion. In *Proc. 20th ACM SIGKDD Int. Conf. on Knowledge Discovery and Data Mining*. ACM, pages 601–610.

Arnab Dutta, Christian Meilicke, and Simone Paolo Ponzetto. 2014. A probabilistic approach for integrating heterogeneous knowledge sources. In *European Semantic Web Conf.*. Springer, pages 286–301.

Christiane Fellbaum, editor. 1998. *WordNet: An Electronic Lexical Database*. MIT Press, Cambridge, MA.

Eibe Frank, Mark A. Hall, and Ian H. Witten. 2016. *Data Mining: Practical Machine Learning Tools and Techniques*, Morgan Kaufmann, chapter The WEKA Workbench. 4th edition.

Taher H Haveliwala. 2002. Topic-sensitive pagerank. In *Proc. 11th int. World Wide Web Conf.*. ACM, pages 517–526.

Jerónimo Hernández-González, Iñaki Inza, and Jose A. Lozano. 2016. Weak supervision and other non-standard classification problems: a taxonomy. *Pattern Recognit. Lett.* 69:49–55.

Ni Lao and William W. Cohen. 2010. Relational retrieval using a combination of path-constrained random walks. *Mach. Learn.* 81(1):53–67.

T. Mitchell, W. Cohen, E. Hruschka, P. Talukdar, J. Betteridge, A. Carlson, B. Dalvi, M. Gardner, B. Kisiel, J. Krishnamurthy, N. Lao, K. Mazaitis, T. Mohamed, N. Nakashole, E. Platanios, A. Ritter, M. Samadi, B. Settles, R. Wang, D. Wijaya, A. Gupta, X. Chen, A. Saparov, M. Greaves, and J. Welling. 2015. Never-ending learning. In *Proc. 29th AAAI Conf. Artificial Intelligence (AAAI)*.

Lawrence Page, Sergey Brin, Rajeev Motwani, and Terry Winograd. 1999. The pagerank citation ranking: Bringing order to the web. Tech. Report 1999-66, Stanford InfoLab.

Fabian M Suchanek, Gjergji Kasneci, and Gerhard Weikum. 2008. Yago: A large ontology from wikipedia and wordnet. *J. Web Semant.* 6(3):203–217.

D. T. Wijaya and T. Mitchell. 2016. Mapping verbs in different languages to knowledge base relations using web text as interlingua. In *Proc. 15th Annu. Conf. North Am. Chapter Assoc. Comput. Linguist.: Hum. Lang. Technol. (NAACL)*.

Parameter Free Hierarchical Graph-Based Clustering for Analyzing Continuous Word Embeddings

Thomas A. Trost   **Dietrich Klakow**

Saarland University

Saarbrücken, Germany

{thomas.trost,dietrich.klakow}@lsv.uni-saarland.de

Abstract

Word embeddings are high-dimensional vector representations of words and are thus difficult to interpret. In order to deal with this, we introduce an unsupervised parameter free method for creating a hierarchical graphical clustering of the full ensemble of word vectors and show that this structure is a geometrically meaningful representation of the original relations between the words. This newly obtained representation can be used for better understanding and thus improving the embedding algorithm and exhibits semantic meaning, so it can also be utilized in a variety of language processing tasks like categorization or measuring similarity.

1 Introduction

There are different ways to assess word embeddings (Yaghoobzadeh and Schütze, 2016). While some authors focus on general properties, as for example Levy et al. (2015) or Hashimoto et al. (2016), most evaluations are with respect to specific tasks. Examples of the latter include the works by Baroni et al. (2014), Schnabel et al. (2015), or Rothe and Schütze (2016), to name but a few. The objective of this paper is to introduce a method for getting a grasp of the *global* structure of embeddings, which is different from general schemes for dimensionality reduction like t-SNE (Maaten and Hinton, 2008), the methods summarized by Van Der Maaten et al. (2009), or visualization interfaces such as Roleo (Sayeed et al., 2016) and GoWvis (Tixier et al., 2016). The method presented here is a specific way of clustering (a field nicely reviewed by Jain et al. (1999)) that works particularly well for the current objective.

We present a global analysis of the statistical properties of the embedding space. This is based on the output of the well-known word2vec program (Mikolov et al., 2013), using the example of the dataset published alongside the source code on the web[1], which was generated with the skip-gram model with negative sampling. This dataset was trained on parts of the English Google news corpus and consists of 3,000,000 words with 300-dimensional embedding vectors. First, densities in the embedding space will be explored. Based on that a parameter free hierarchical graph-based clustering approach is developed that is the basis of a tool that allows to explore the neighborhood of a term of interest.

The paper is structured as follows: After a quick discussion of statistical properties of the dataset, the concept of the graphical neighborhood hierarchy is explained. Specific properties of the resulting graphs are brought into the context of peculiarities of the dataset for showing that this representation is particularly well-suited. Finally, the semantic properties of the graphs are briefly evaluated.

2 Properties of Embedding Spaces

First, a look at global statistics of the dataset lays a basis for justifying later choices and interpreting the hierarchy. Herein, special care must be taken with respect to effects of the high dimensionality.

The distribution of the values of single vector components all look very similar and peak clearly at the origin, but they exhibit relatively heavy tails. The distribution of the L_2-norm[2] of the embedding vectors can be seen in fig. 1, both for all and rare words, where the latter are those that are not found

---

[1] https://code.google.com/archive/p/word2vec/

[2] For a discussion of the choice of distance function, see section 3.2 below.

Proceedings of TextGraphs-11: the Workshop on Graph-based Methods for Natural Language Processing, ACL 2017, pages 30–38,
Vancouver, Canada, August 3, 2017. ©2017 Association for Computational Linguistics

in the *1 billion word* corpus (Chelba et al., 2013). Even though the curves show a drop at the origin

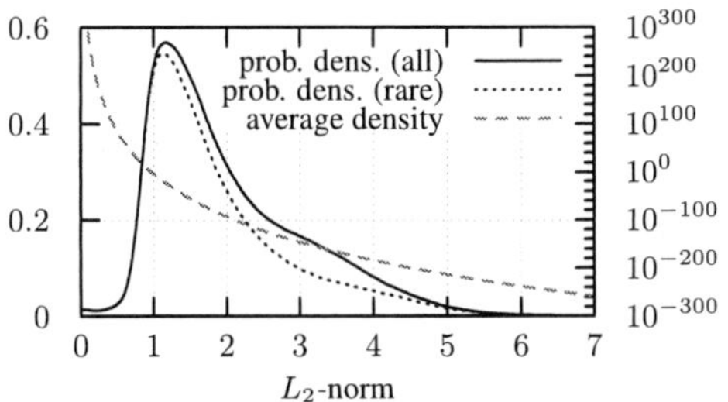

Figure 1: *Probability densities* for finding a word vector with the given norm, for all and rare words (left axis, density for rare words rescaled for reflecting proportion) and plot of the resulting *average density* at the respective distance to the origin (right axis).

and a clear peak at slightly above one, they are mostly a consequence of the high dimensionality of the embedding space. This becomes apparent in the plot of the actual average density (words per volume) at a given distance from the origin (also fig. 1), which decreases very rapidly and monotonically. It can be concluded that embedding vectors are highly concentrated around the origin, but that common words tend to lie at an intermediate distance to the origin and do not fully follow the general distribution.

Next, a principle component analysis can be done in order to evaluate how isotropic the dataset actually is. It reveals that the largest and smallest eigenvalues are only about an order of magnitude apart and that the top 20 percent of eigenvalues account for roughly 50 percent of the total variance in the dataset. While this is clearly not fully isotropic, there appear to be no directions that are completely superfluous. For the global picture, approximate isotropy is thus a fairly reasonable assumption.

To complete the general statistical exploration of the embedding space we want to look at specific word classes (common nouns, verbs and adjectives) versus other words that belong to none of these classes. We also want to explore the impact of the word frequency on the position in the embedding space. Figure 2 gives the results. The first – however non-surprising – observation is that the center of the embedding space is made up of low frequency words that are not nouns, verbs or adjectives. These three POS classes densely popu-

late the surface of a 300 dimensional sphere in a distance of three to four from the center of the embedding space. Exploring this rim in more detail is most interesting for applications. For this we will develop a parameter free method to study the vicinity of a word of interest to the user of the tool.

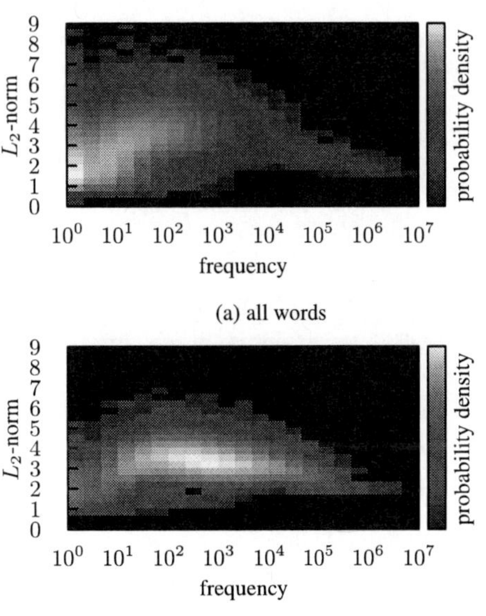

(a) all words

(b) common nouns, verbs, and adjectives

Figure 2: Probability density for finding an embedding vector of a word of given frequency and a given L_2-norm and thus distance from the origin. Note that the density is given in log-scale.

3 Nearest Neighbor Graph

Consider a set of embedding vectors $\mathcal{W}$ that is equipped with a distance function $d : \mathcal{W} \times \mathcal{W} \to \mathbb{R}_0^+$. The *nearest neighbor graph* (NNG) on $\mathcal{W}$ is a directed weighted graph where each vertex v has outdegree one and is connected to its nearest neighbor $w = \arg\min_{w'} d(v, w')$, with the weight corresponding to the distance. In case of ambiguity, the nearest neighbor has to be selected via additional criteria or randomly. Note that the nearest neighbor relation need not be reciprocal. The k-NNG which incorporates the notion of k nearest neighbors can be defined in a similar way, but it lacks most of the nice properties of the simple NNG, some of which will be discussed next.

Naive implementations for nearest neighbor search scale quadratically with the number $n = |\mathcal{W}|$ of nodes, however, $\mathcal{O}(n \log n)$-solutions are available (Sankaranarayanan et al., 2007), whose efficiency depends on the dimensionality of $\mathcal{W}$. Thus, in particular for high-dimensional spaces, approximate nearest neighbor search may be much more efficient (Muja and Lowe, 2009).

3.1 Clusters

Here, the weakly connected components of an NNG are denoted as *clusters*. That is to say, there is a path between every two vertices within a cluster, if the direction of the edges is ignored. It can readily be seen that each cluster must have exactly one cluster root, which is a pair of vertices that see each other as their nearest neighbor. Apart from that, there cannot be any cycles in a cluster, so it can be considered as two trees each of which is rooted in one vertex of the cluster root. This tree-like and very clear structure of the clusters makes them interesting for our purposes. Example clusters extracted from the NNG of the `word2vec` dataset are depicted in fig. 5, which will be discussed below.

3.2 Choice of Distance Function

The particular choice of a distance function d may drastically affect the form of an NNG. In general, it is advantageous if d has the properties of an actual metric, because then it corresponds closely to the human notion of a distance which makes it easier to interpret the results.

For a variety of additional reasons, here, the classical Euclidean distance

$$d_{\mathrm{E}}(v, w) := \sqrt{\sum_i (v_i - w_i)^2} \qquad (1)$$

is chosen. Most importantly, d_{E} is invariant under orthogonal transformations (rotating and flipping), which goes well with the apparent isotropy of the embedding space. With this distance function, no particular component or direction is given more attention than another. Besides that, the Euclidean distance is relatively cheap and easy to compute and there is a lot of literature on specialized methods for finding NNGs with this metric. Furthermore, d_{E} is loosely related to the cosine similarity that is used as the main ingredient during the training of the embedding mapping.

4 Neighborhood Hierarchy

By means of an NNG, the local structure between the words within each of its clusters can be understood fairly well, but any information about

the relationship between different clusters is completely lost. In order to deal with that, the simple NNG can be extended via a *neighborhood hierarchy* (NH), which adds information about the neighborhood relation between clusters, clusters of cluster and so on. A sketch of the first two levels of such a hierarchy is given in fig. 3. Each cluster is equipped with what could be called a *macro vertex*, which might for example be the mean of the vertices in the cluster, the center of the cluster root, or the most frequent (and thus hopefully most important) word in the cluster. Then the NNG of the macro vertices can be determined. This leads to new clusters, new macro vertices, another NNG and so forth, till the top level is reached, which contains only one cluster of macro vertices. In order to make the whole hierarchy browsable, the macro vertices can be given a clearer meaning by assigning one representative word to each of them. This word might for example be the nearest one to the macro vertex or the most frequent word in the cluster.

While the nearest neighbor relationship alone is somewhat problematic, as small changes in the dataset may result in huge differences in the cluster layout (in particular in high-dimensional spaces), the hierarchy smooths this effect away to some degree, as lower-level flipping between clusters will probably not affect higher level clusters.

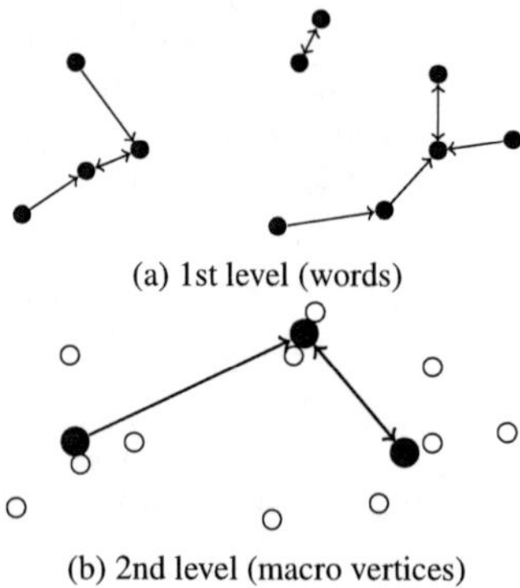

(a) 1st level (words)

(b) 2nd level (macro vertices)

Figure 3: Sketch of a cluster hierarchy. The massive dots are the centers of mass of the clusters of small dots and form a cluster themselves.

5 Hierarchy of Vector Embeddings

The method from the previous section can now be applied to the set of embedding vectors. The word vectors form clusters and the macro vertices introduced above can be seen as generic or in some way paraphrasing terms for the words in their cluster (see section 6 for semantic evaluation), under the given premise that similar words are mapped to nearby vectors. The NH produces a partitioning of the vector space in the spirit of a Voronoi diagram at various levels of coarseness and can thus be used to navigate through the otherwise hard to grasp high-dimensional space.

5.1 General Properties of the Hierarchy

The NH of the `word2vec` dataset has a total of six levels. The first level contains the words themselves, higher levels comprise macro vertices as described above. General properties of the graphs on the different levels are given in table 1. In accordance with the hierarchical structure, the number of words and thus the number of clusters decrease exponentially.

Typical characteristics of the graphs are strongly influenced by the fact that the graphs are NNGs. As each cluster has one root and each of the n vertices has out-degree one, the *reciprocity*

$$r := \frac{\#\text{reciprocal edges}}{n} \qquad (2)$$

is proportional to the inverse of the average number of words per cluster. The more elaborate measure of reciprocity ρ introduced by Garlaschelli and Loffredo (2004) reduces to

$$\rho = \frac{r(n-1)-1}{n-2} \underset{n \gg 1}{\approx} r \qquad (3)$$

and is thus almost the same as r for the larger graphs. Note that the expression (3) is not defined for the sixth level. ρ is rather low compared to other natural networks, but interestingly it lies just in the range of other word networks (Garlaschelli and Loffredo, 2004).

Here, the depth d of the graphs for a specific leaf is the number of edges between the leaf and the respective cluster root. The average of d over all leafs and the maximum value of d are presented in table 1. While $\max(d)$ decreases exponentially, possibly in accordance with the shrinking of the cluster size, particularly the constancy of the mid-level $\varnothing d$ is striking and a sign of two contrary processes. The longer connections on the lower levels are compensated for by more small connections, or, in other words, the smaller high-level clusters are more regular in terms of their depths.

On all levels, the NNGs appear to be scale free (Barabási and Bonabeau, 2003), with the con-

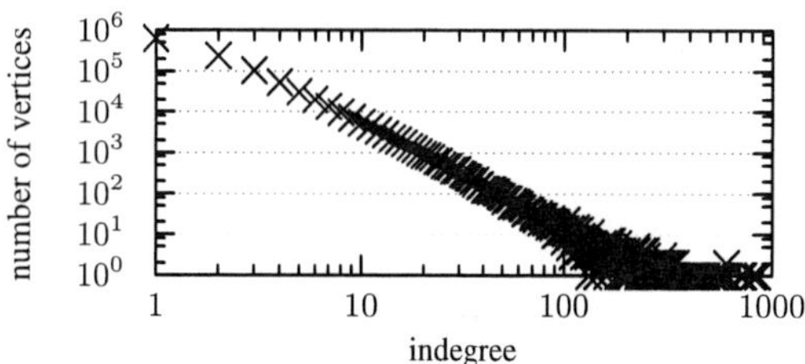

Figure 4: Log-log scatter plot of the number of times a first-level vertex has a particular indegree. While this point cannot be represented in the chart, there are about 1.8×10^6 vertices with an indegree of 0 in the NNG.

level	1	2	3	4	5	6
# words	$3{\cdot}10^6$	99,884	6750	540	55	2
# clusters	99,884	6750	540	55	2	1
$\varnothing$ w./cl.	30.0	14.8	12.5	9.8	27.5	2.0
r	0.067	0.14	0.16	0.20	0.073	1.0
ρ	0.067	0.14	0.16	0.20	0.055	–
$\varnothing d$	6.6	2.5	2.5	2.5	2.4	–
$\max(d)$	25	16	10	6	4	–

Table 1: General properties of the NH of the `word2vec` dataset. In the third row, the average number of words per cluster is given. See section 5.1 for definitions of the other quantities.

straint that the higher-level graphs contain too little vertices for making a definite statement about that. Exemplarily, this feature can be seen for the first-level graph in fig. 4. Scale freeness is primarily associated to processes in which new vertices are attached preferably to those existing vertices that already have a large indegree. In the current context this sheds a light on the behavior of the learning algorithm, specifically because scale freeness is encountered on all levels. A possible interpretation is that the algorithm leads to a multi-level attaching of words and groups of words while trying to put similar words as close to each other as possible. Interestingly, different semantic networks exhibit the scale-free property, too (Steyvers and Tenenbaum, 2005).

5.2 Examples of Clusters

Examples of first-level clusters extracted from the `word2vec` dataset can be found in fig. 5. At this point, only the surface can be scratched, because there are thousands of such clusters and many of them are interesting in some way.

The dataset contains a pretty raw set of words;

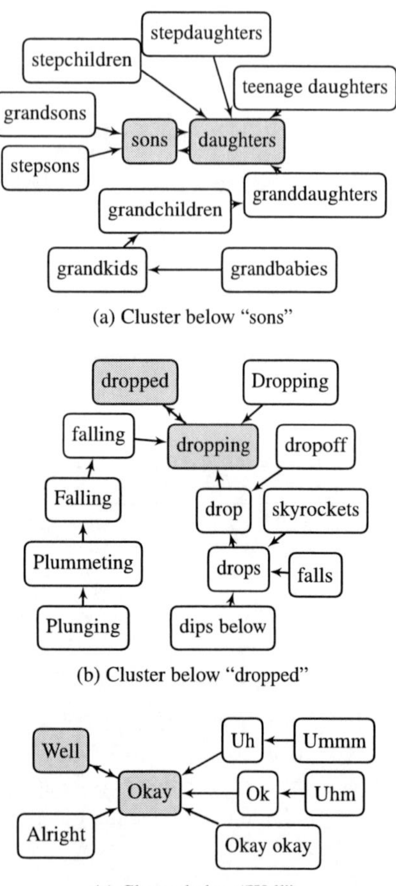

(a) Cluster below "sons"

(b) Cluster below "dropped"

(c) Cluster below "Well"

Figure 5: Example clusters from actual dataset, with cluster roots marked gray. The most frequent word of the cluster is chosen as the macro vertex and given in the description.

proper names, capitalized or inflected words, misspellings, or fillers have not been stripped from the data. From the context-based training method (Mikolov et al., 2013) it can be expected that syntactically similar words end up close to each other, which is indeed seen in the NH, as in fig. 5c, where fillers and certain discourse items, all of them capitalized, form a cluster. This might also explain that only plural forms have gathered in fig. 5a. While this often means that connected items are also semantically similar, antonyms like "drops" and "skyrockets" in fig. 5b are frequently close to each other due to their similar syntactic roles. Despite such problems, it must be stressed that fig. 5 is not the result of extensive cherry picking, but that semantically meaningful clusters are the rule, even if the large number of proper names and

more or less meaningless padding words sometimes shadow the more interesting clusters.

After this glance at some first-level clusters, an example of the actual hierarchy is shown in fig. 6. On the lowest levels, the words are closely related to their neighbors and the words in their parent clusters, just as it has been the case in fig. 5. This is still the case on the next levels, but, in general, the higher one gets in the hierarchy, the looser the connection to the words on the lower levels, because a lot of words are collected beneath a specific high-level word and not all of them can be equally suitable. In the specific situation in fig. 6, the words on the third level are mostly related to finance and economy and the same accounts for the fourth level, with more and more rather unspecific words in between. Revealing this is just what the hierarchy is good for: The fact that "index"-related words are collected in the "financial region" of the embedding space is not self-evident. If the embeddings would not have been trained on a news corpus but on scientific resources, the position of the word "index" would very likely be a different one.

Here, the primary purpose of the NH is getting a better understanding of embeddings and the meaning of the relations in the NH must therefore not be over-interpreted, because they explicitly have to be left as unaltered as possible for making them good representatives of the raw dataset. Specific relations can often (see below) but not necessarily be transferred into a semantic order, as can exemplarily be seen in fig. 5a, where kinship relations are not organized as one would probably put them. However, this is what the dataset looks like in terms of geometrical neighborhood. If certain words are positioned in a different way from what could be expected, this does not mean that the clustering went wrong, but rather that something interesting happened in the embedding space.

5.3 Geometry of Clusters

The neighborhood relation gives a good view of the relative positioning of the words, but the geometry of the clusters and their orientation in the vector space is mostly veiled. Luckily, certain statistics reveal that there is much regularity in the shape of the clusters, so that the cluster alone contains enough information for telling where a specific word is likely to be found.

For each pair of embedding vector v and the

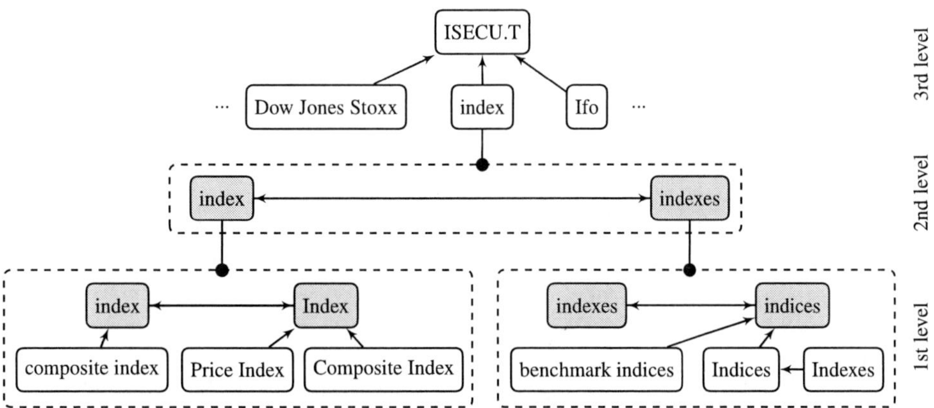

Figure 6: Example of relations between clusters on the three lowest levels of the hierarchy. The dashed boxes frame clusters. Note that only an excerpt of the (much larger) cluster on the third level is shown. Lines ending in a circle indicate the connection between macro vertices and their clusters.

respective nearest neighbor w, the *radiality* $R \in [-1, 1]$ of this nearest neighbor relation can be defined as the normalized scalar product between v and the difference vector between w and v via

$$R := \frac{v \cdot (w - v)}{|v||w - v|}. \qquad (4)$$

Positive values of R mean, that w lies farther away from the origin than v, while negative values imply the opposite. In fig. 7, the probability density for finding a certain value for R is shown. It can be

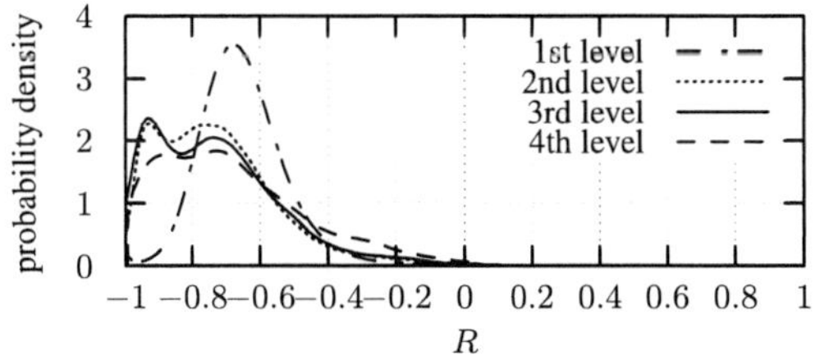

Figure 7: Radiality R, as defined in (4).

concluded that for the data at hand, the neighborhood relation on all levels strongly tends to point "inward", i.e. towards the origin of the embedding space. In other words, it is almost certain, that the nearest neighbor of a word vector lies closer to the origin of the coordinate system than the word vector itself. On this basis and as the clusters are basically trees that grow away from the cluster root, it can be expected that the cluster roots typically lie near to the origin, compared to the other vertices in the respective cluster. This can be checked by plotting the probability density for finding a

cluster with a given percentage of vertices that are farther away from the origin than the cluster root (Figure 8). As expected, in most clusters the ma-

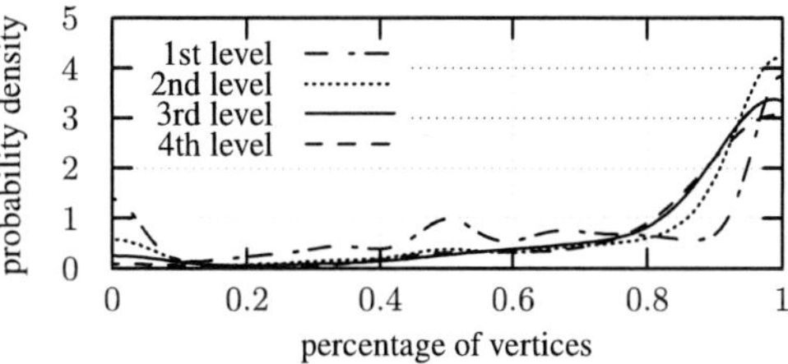

Figure 8: Probability density for finding clusters where the given percentage of vertices lie farther away from the origin than the cluster root.

jority of vertices tends to lie farther outside than the cluster root. Nevertheless, the probability density shows little bumps around fractions of small integers like $\frac{1}{3}$, $\frac{1}{2}$, or $\frac{2}{3}$. These are mostly due to small clusters, for which the position of the cluster root within the cluster seems to be less predictable. However, these clusters contain only a small fraction of all words and their structure is easy to understand anyway. If only relatively large clusters are taken into account, the probability density peaks much more strongly around the value 1.

Taking all this into account, and even though there is no notion of geometry in the NNG, the meaning of clusters like those in fig. 5 becomes much more transparent: The root is very likely the closest vertex to the origin and the other vertices are successively farther outside. For example, the representation vectors of the words "falling",

"Falling", "Plummeting", and "Plunging" have an increasing L_2-norm or distance from the origin and they form a chain in the graph in fig. 5b. Only a bit additional information about the position of the root is thus sufficient for getting an idea of the position and orientation of the whole cluster.

6   Evaluation

The focus of this paper is on the analysis of embeddings. Nevertheless, as already mentioned above, the findings presented in the previous sections indicate that the NH might be used for NLP tasks beyond visualization of word embeddings or other large high-dimensional datasets, because the neighborhood and macro vertex relations appear to be connected to semantical relations between the words, particularly on the lower levels. Possible tasks that directly come to mind are measuring relatedness or similarity, various kinds of tagging, and classification. In contrast to typical semantical frameworks like *WordNet* (Miller, 1995) or *FrameNet* (Baker et al., 1998) whose creation requires extensive human resources, the NH can be created without expert knowledge in a very short time and has the capability of including much more words.

Zesch and Gurevych (2007) analyze graphs extracted from Wikipedia[3] and summarize a variety of methods for evaluating semantic relations. In this spirit and for a first and quick quantitative view at the NH, similarity between neighbors in the graph and between words and their macro vertex are tested by calculating the respective Wu-Palmer similarity scores (Wu and Palmer, 1994) on *WordNet* (Miller, 1995). Other scores basically lead to similar results and are thus not discussed in more detail. Because the number of words in *WordNet* is much smaller than that in the dataset under consideration, the analysis is limited to those words that can be found in both datasets, which amounts to 54,586 words. For that to be possible, a NH of these words alone is used, which is distinct from the full hierarchy discussed above. The usefulness of these results for a much smaller dataset can be justified by envisioning that the sparser NNG must roughly be a skeleton of the full graph for geometrical reasons and must thus be related to the latter. Besides that, quantifying similarity on the smaller graph is interesting in its own right.

____
[3]http://www.wikipedia.org

The results for the first four levels of the NH are shown in fig. 9. Intuitively, the semantic relations between neighbors or words and macro vertices are expected to be stronger, if more "probability mass" can be found on the right side of the plot, because then more relations correspond to a higher similarity. In order to clarify the meaning of the curves, a baseline curve is added that corresponds to an equivalent evaluation of random word pairs.

Both the neighborhood relation and the macro vertex assignment yield noticeably better results than the baseline. In accordance with earlier remarks, the curves confirm that the semantical significance of the hierarchy is much higher on the lower levels. While the first and the second level appear to exhibit a large amount of meaningful relations, the higher levels are not much better than the baseline.

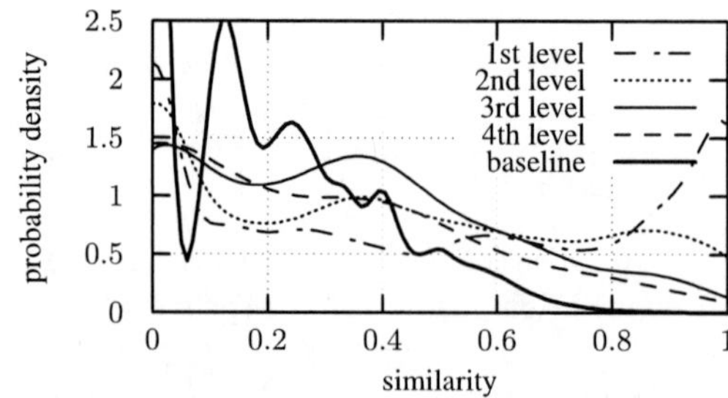

(a) Similarity between words and their neighbors

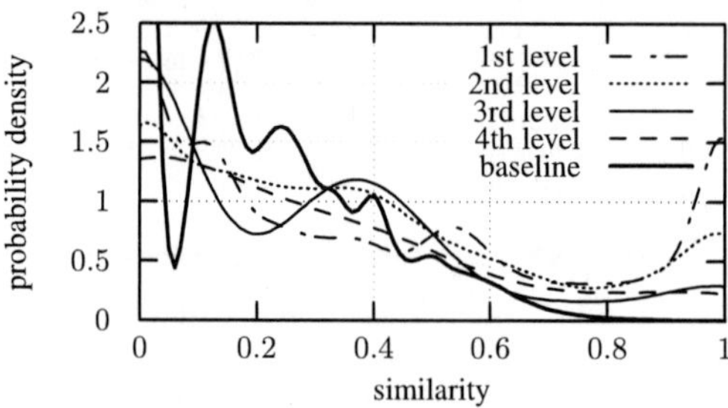

(b) Similarity between words and their macro vertices

Figure 9: Evaluation of similarity. The curves represent the probability density of finding a certain Wu-Palmer similarity between the respective words. The baseline peaks at (0,6.8) but is cut off for clarity of the other curves.

7   Conclusion and Outlook

In this paper we have presented a general graph-based method for the analysis of embedding spaces. At the heart lies a neighborhood hierarchy (NH), a parameter free, flexible and general concept for clustering data in arbitrary spaces, which eliminates the problem of interpreting high-dimensional vectors while preserving the most important geometric information. In order to get a better understanding of the data, a variety of statistical properties of word embeddings has been evaluated. First evidence of the semantic significance of the NH has been established by relating it to WordNet data.

This method of analysis will allow researchers to interactively explore the neighborhood relations in an embedding space. This will enable them not only to get a better intuition of the structure of embedding spaces but will also give them new ideas on how to incorporate embeddings in natural language processing tasks like information extraction or other tasks that require semantic knowledge.

Acknowledgments

This work was funded by the Deutsche Forschungsgemeinschaft (DFG) under grant SFB 1102.

References

Collin F. Baker, Charles J. Fillmore, and John B. Lowe. 1998. The Berkeley FrameNet Project. In *Proceedings of the 36th Annual Meeting of the Association for Computational Linguistics and 17th International Conference on Computational Linguistics, Volume 1*. Association for Computational Linguistics, Montreal, Quebec, Canada, pages 86–90. https://doi.org/10.3115/980845.980860.

Albert-László Barabási and Eric Bonabeau. 2003. Scale-free networks. *Scientific American* 288(5):60–69. https://doi.org/10.1038/scientificamerican0503-60.

Marco Baroni, Georgiana Dinu, and Germán Kruszewski. 2014. Don't count, predict! A systematic comparison of context-counting vs. context-predicting semantic vectors. In *Proceedings of the 52nd Annual Meeting of the Association for Computational Linguistics (Volume 1: Long Papers)*. Association for Computational Linguistics, Baltimore, Maryland, pages 238–247. http://www.aclweb.org/anthology/P14-1023.

Ciprian Chelba, Tomas Mikolov, Mike Schuster, Qi Ge, Thorsten Brants, and Phillipp Koehn. 2013. One Billion Word Benchmark for Measuring Progress in Statistical Language Modeling. *CoRR* abs/1312.3005. http://arxiv.org/abs/1312.3005.

Diego Garlaschelli and Maria I. Loffredo. 2004. Patterns of Link Reciprocity in Directed Networks. *Physical Review Letters* 93(26). https://doi.org/10.1103/physrevlett.93.268701.

Tatsunori Hashimoto, David Alvarez-Melis, and Tommi Jaakkola. 2016. Word Embeddings as Metric Recovery in Semantic Spaces. *Transactions of the Association for Computational Linguistics* 4:273–286. https://transacl.org/ojs/index.php/tacl/article/view/809.

Anil K. Jain, M. Narasimha Murty, and Patrick J. Flynn. 1999. Data Clustering: A Review. *ACM computing surveys (CSUR)* 31(3):264–323. https://doi.org/10.1145/331499.331504.

Omer Levy, Yoav Goldberg, and Ido Dagan. 2015. Improving distributional similarity with lessons learned from word embeddings. *Transactions of the Association for Computational Linguistics* 3:211–225. https://transacl.org/ojs/index.php/tacl/article/view/570.

Laurens van der Maaten and Geoffrey Hinton. 2008. Visualizing data using t-SNE. *Journal of Machine Learning Research* 9(Nov):2579–2605.

Tomas Mikolov, Ilya Sutskever, Kai Chen, Greg S Corrado, and Jeff Dean. 2013. Distributed representations of words and phrases and their compositionality. In *Advances in Neural Information Processing Systems*. pages 3111–3119.

George A. Miller. 1995. WordNet: A Lexical Database for English. *Communications of the ACM* 38(11):39–41. https://doi.org/10.1145/219717.219748.

Marius Muja and David G. Lowe. 2009. Fast approximate nearest neighbors with automatic algorithm configuration. *Proceedings of the Conference on Computer Vision Theory and Applications (VISAPP) (1)* 2(331-340):2. https://doi.org/10.1.1.160.1721.

Sascha Rothe and Hinrich Schütze. 2016. Word Embedding Calculus in Meaningful Ultradense Subspaces. In *Proceedings of the 54th Annual Meeting of the Association for Computational Linguistics (Volume 2: Short Papers)*. Association for Computational Linguistics, Berlin, Germany, pages 512–517. http://anthology.aclweb.org/P16-2083.

Jagan Sankaranarayanan, Hanan Samet, and Amitabh Varshney. 2007. A fast all nearest neighbor algorithm for applications involving large point-clouds. *Computers & Graphics* 31(2):157–174. https://doi.org/10.1016/j.cag.2006.11.011.

Asad Sayeed, Xudong Hong, and Vera Demberg. 2016. Roleo: Visualising thematic fit spaces on the web. In *Proceedings of ACL-2016 System Demonstrations*. Association for Computational Linguistics, Berlin, Germany, pages 139–144. http://anthology.aclweb.org/P16-4024.

Tobias Schnabel, Igor Labutov, David Mimno, and Thorsten Joachims. 2015. Evaluation methods for unsupervised word embeddings. In *Proceedings of the 2015 Conference on Empirical Methods in Natural Language Processing*. Association for Computational Linguistics, Lisbon, Portugal, pages 298–307. http://aclweb.org/anthology/D15-1036.

Mark Steyvers and Joshua B. Tenenbaum. 2005. The Large-scale structure of semantic networks: Statistical analyses and a model of semantic growth. *Cognitive Science* 29(1):41–78.

Antoine Tixier, Konstantinos Skianis, and Michalis Vazirgiannis. 2016. GoWvis: A Web Application for Graph-of-Words-based Text Visualization and Summarization. In *Proceedings of ACL-2016 System Demonstrations*. Association for Computational Linguistics, Berlin, Germany, pages 151–156. http://anthology.aclweb.org/P16-4026.

Laurens Van Der Maaten, Eric Postma, and Jaap Van den Herik. 2009. Dimensionality Reduction: A Comparative Review. *Journal of Machine Learning Research* 10:66–71.

Zhibiao Wu and Martha Palmer. 1994. Verb Semantics and Lexical Selection. In *Proceedings of the 32nd Annual Meeting of the Association for Computational Linguistics*. Association for Computational Linguistics, Las Cruces, New Mexico, USA, pages 133–138. https://doi.org/10.3115/981732.981751.

Yadollah Yaghoobzadeh and Hinrich Schütze. 2016. Intrinsic Subspace Evaluation of Word Embedding Representations. In *Proceedings of the 54th Annual Meeting of the Association for Computational Linguistics (Volume 1: Long Papers)*. Association for Computational Linguistics, Berlin, Germany, pages 236–246. http://www.aclweb.org/anthology/P16-1023.

Torsten Zesch and Iryna Gurevych. 2007. Analysis of the Wikipedia category graph for NLP applications. In *Proceedings of the TextGraphs-2 Workshop (NAACL-HLT 2007)*. pages 1–8.

Spectral Graph-Based Method of Multimodal Word Embedding [*]

Kazuki Fukui[♠♡] and **Takamasa Oshikiri**[◇♡] and **Hidetoshi Shimodaira**[♠♡]
♠ Department of Systems Science, Graduate School of Informatics, Kyoto University
♡ Mathematical Statistics Team, RIKEN Center for Advanced Intelligence Project
◇ Division of Mathematical Science, Graduate School of Engineering Science, Osaka University
`k.fukui@sys.i.kyoto-u.ac.jp`
`oshikiri@sigmath.es.osaka-u.ac.jp`
`shimo@i.kyoto-u.ac.jp`

Abstract

In this paper, we propose a novel method for multimodal word embedding, which exploit a generalized framework of multi-view spectral graph embedding to take into account visual appearances or scenes denoted by words in a corpus. We evaluated our method through word similarity tasks and a concept-to-image search task, having found that it provides word representations that reflect visual information, while somewhat trading-off the performance on the word similarity tasks. Moreover, we demonstrate that our method captures multimodal linguistic regularities, which enable recovering relational similarities between words and images by vector arithmetic.

1 Introduction

Word embedding plays important roles in the field of Natural Language Processing (NLP). Many existing studies use word vectors for various downstream NLP tasks, such as text classification, Part-of-Speech tagging, and machine translation. One of the most famous approaches is skip-gram model (Mikolov et al., 2013), which is based on a neural network, and its extensions have also been widely studied as well.

There are alternative approaches depending on a spectral graph embedding framework (Yan et al., 2007; Huang et al., 2012) for word embedding. For examples, Dhillon et al. (2015) proposed a method based on Canonical Correlation Analysis (CCA) (Hotelling, 1936), while a PCA based word embedding method was proposed in Lebret and Collobert (2014).

In recent years, many researchers have been actively studying the use of multiple modalities in the fields of both NLP and computer vision. Those studies combine textual and visual information to propose methods for image-caption matching (Yan and Mikolajczyk, 2015), caption generation (Kiros et al., 2014), visual question answering (Antol et al., 2015), quantifying abstractness (Kiela et al., 2014) of words, and so on.

As for word embedding, multimodal versions of word2vec (Mikolov et al., 2013) have been proposed in Lazaridou et al. (2015) and Kottur et al. (2016). The first one jointly optimize the objective of both skip-gram model and a cross-modal objective across texts and images, and the latter uses abstract scenes as surrogate labels for capturing visually grounded semantic relatedness. More recently, Mao et al. (2016) proposed a multimodal word embedding methods based on a recurrent neural network to learn word vectors from their newly proposed large scale image caption dataset.

In this paper, we introduce a new spectral graph-based method of multimodal word embedding. Specifically, we extend Eigenwords (Dhillon et al., 2015), a CCA-based method for word embedding, by applying a generalized framework of spectral graph embedding (Nori et al., 2012; Shimodaira, 2016). Figure 1 shows a schematic diagram of our method.

In the rest of this paper, we call our method **Multimodal Eigenwords** (MM-Eigenwords). The most similar existing method is Multimodal Skip-gram model (MMskip-gram) (Lazaridou et al., 2015), which slightly differ in that our model can easily deal with many-to-many relationships between words in a corpus and their relevant images, while MMskip-gram only considers one-to-one relationships between concrete words and images.

Using a corpus and datasets of image-word rela-

* This work was partially supported by grants from Japan Society for the Promotion of Science KAKENHI (16H02789) to HS.

Proceedings of TextGraphs-11: the Workshop on Graph-based Methods for Natural Language Processing, ACL 2017, pages 39–44,
Vancouver, Canada, August 3, 2017. ©2017 Association for Computational Linguistics

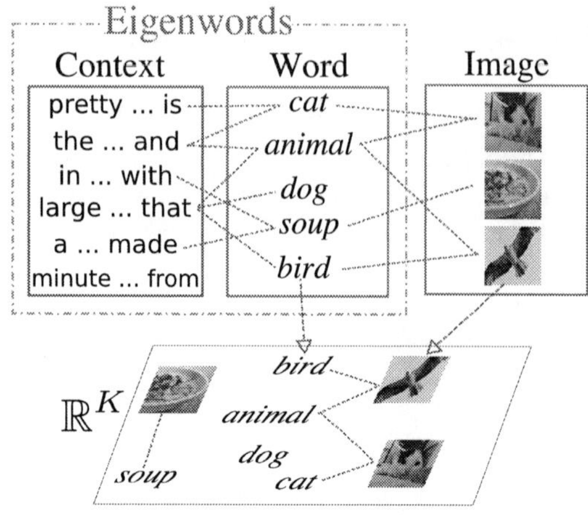

Figure 1: Our proposed method extends a CCA-based method of word embedding by means of multi-view spectral graph embedding frameworks of dimensionality reduction to deal with visual information associated with words in a corpus.

tionships, which are available in common benchmark datasets or on online photo sharing services, MM-Eigenwords jointly learns word vectors on a common multimodal space and a linear mapping from a visual feature space to the multimodal space. Those word vectors also reflect similarities between words and images.

We evaluated the multimodal word representations obtained by our model through word similarity task and concept-to-image search, having found that our model has ability to capture both semantic and word-to-image similarities. We also found that our model captures multimodal linguistic regularities (Kiros et al., 2014), whose examples are shown in Figure 2b.

2 Multi-view Spectral Graph Embedding

A spectral graph perspective of dimensionality reduction was first proposed in Yan et al. (2007), which showed that several major statistical methods for dimensionality reduction, such as PCA and Eigenmap (Belkin and Niyogi, 2003), can be written in a form of graph embedding frameworks, where data points are nodes and those points have weighted links between other points. Huang et al. (2012) extended this work for two-view data with many-to-many relationships (or links) and showed that their two-view graph embedding framework includes CCA, one of the most popular method for multi-view data analysis, as its special cases.

However, available datasets may have more than two views with complex graph structures, which are unmanageable for CCA or Multiset CCA (Kettenring, 1971) whose inputs must be fed in the form of n-tuples.

Shimodaira (2016) further generalized the graph embedding frameworks to deal with many-to-many relationships between any number of views, and Nori et al. (2012) also proposed an equivalent method for multimodal relation prediction in social data. This generalized framework is used to extend Eigenwords for cross-lingual word embedding (Oshikiri et al., 2016), where vocabularies and contexts of multiple languages are linked through sentence-level alignment. Our proposed method also makes use of the framework of Shimodaira (2016) to extend Eigenwords for multimodal word embedding.

3 Eigenwords (One Step CCA)

Canonical Correlation Analysis (Hotelling, 1936) is a multivariate analysis method for finding optimal projections of two sets of data vectors by maximizing the correlations. Applying CCA to pairs of raw word vectors and raw context vectors, Eigenwords algorithms attempt to find low-dimensional vector representations of words (Dhillon et al., 2015). Here we explain the simplest version of Eigenwords called One Step CCA (OSCCA).

We have a corpus consisting of T tokens; $(t_i)_{i=1,...,T}$, and the vocabulary consisting of V word types; $\{v_i\}_{i=1,...,V}$. Each token t_i is drawn from this vocabulary. We define a word matrix $\mathbf{V} \in \{0, 1\}^{T \times V}$ whose i-th row encodes the token t_i by 1-of-V representation; the j-th element is 1 if the word type of t_i is v_j, 0 otherwise.

Let h be the size of context window. We define context matrix $\mathbf{C} \in \{0, 1\}^{T \times 2hV}$ whose i-th row represents the surrounding context of the token t_i with concatenated 1-of-V encoded vectors of $(t_{i-h}, \ldots, t_{i-1}, t_{i+1}, \ldots, t_{i+h})$.

We apply CCA to T pairs of row vectors of $\mathbf{V}$ and $\mathbf{C}$. The objective function of CCA is constructed using $\mathbf{V}^\top\mathbf{V}$, $\mathbf{V}^\top\mathbf{C}$, $\mathbf{C}^\top\mathbf{C}$ which represent occurrence and co-occurrence counts of words and contexts. In Eigenwords, however, we use $\mathbf{C}_{VV} \in \mathbb{R}_+^{V \times V}$, $\mathbf{C}_{VC} \in \mathbb{R}_+^{V \times 2hV}$, $\mathbf{C}_{CC} \in \mathbb{R}_+^{2hV \times 2hV}$ with the following preprocessing of these matrices before constructing the objective function. First, centering-process of $\mathbf{V}$ and $\mathbf{C}$ is

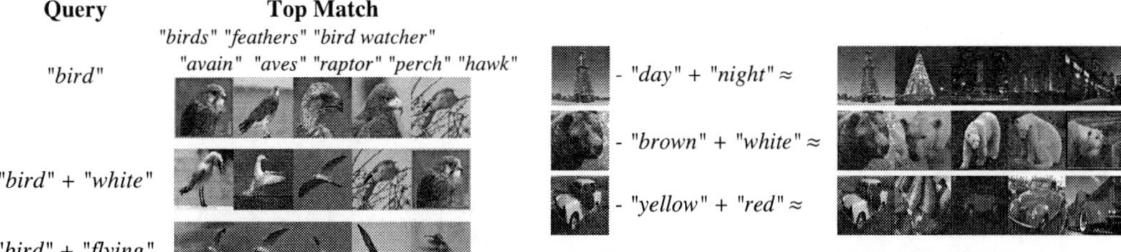

Figure 2: Examples of word-to-image search (a) and demonstrations of vector arithmetics between words and images (b). We chose $\eta = 10^6$ in these examples.

omitted, and off-diagonal elements of $\mathbf{C}^\top\mathbf{C}$ are ignored for simplifying the computation of inverse matrices. Second, we take the square root of the elements of these matrices for "squashing" the heavy-tailed word count distributions. Finally, we obtain vector representations of words as $\mathcal{C}_{VV}^{-1/2}(\boldsymbol{u}_1, \ldots, \boldsymbol{u}_K)$, where $\boldsymbol{u}_1, \ldots, \boldsymbol{u}_K \in \mathbb{R}^V$ are left singular vectors of $\mathcal{C}_{VV}^{-1/2}\,\mathcal{C}_{VC}\,\mathcal{C}_{CC}^{-1/2}$ corresponding to the K largest singular values.

For the fast and scalable computation, Dhillon et al. (2015) employed the method of Halko et al. (2011) which use random projections to compute singular value decomposition of large matrices.

4 Multimodal Eigenwords

In this section, we introduce Multimodal Eigenwords (MM-Eigenwords) by extending the CCA based model of Eigenwords to obtain multimodal representations across words and images.

Suppose we have N_{vis} images, and each image is associated with multiple tags (or words). These associations are denoted by $\tilde{w}_{ij} \geq 0$ ($1 \leq i \leq V, 1 \leq j \leq N_{vis}$), whose value represents the strength of a relationship between the i-th word and the j-th image. In this study, for example, $\tilde{w}_{ij} = 1$ if the j-th image has the i-th word as its tag, whereas $\tilde{w}_{ij} = 0$ otherwise, and we define a matrix $\widetilde{\mathbf{W}}_{VX} = (\tilde{w}_{ij})$. In addition, we denote a image feature matrix by $\mathbf{X}_{vis} \in \mathbb{R}^{N_{vis} \times p_{vis}}$ and its i-th row vector $\boldsymbol{x}_i$, as well as row vectors of $\mathbf{V}, \mathbf{C}$ by $\boldsymbol{v}_i, \boldsymbol{c}_i$ respectively. Here, the goal of MM-Eigenwords is to obtain multimodal representations by extending the CCA in Eigenwords with generalized frameworks of multi-view spectral graph embedding (Nori et al., 2012; Shimodaira, 2016), which include CCA as their special cases. In these frameworks, our goal can be attained by finding an optimal linear mappings to the K-dimensional multimodal space $\mathbf{A}_V, \mathbf{A}_C, \mathbf{A}_{vis}$ that minimize the following objective with a scale constraint.

$$\sum_{i=1}^{T} \|\boldsymbol{v}_i\mathbf{A}_V - \boldsymbol{c}_i\mathbf{A}_C\|_2^2$$

$$+ \sum_{i=1}^{T}\sum_{j=1}^{N_{vis}} \eta w_{ij}\|\boldsymbol{v}_i\mathbf{A}_V - \boldsymbol{x}_j\mathbf{A}_{vis}\|_2^2, \quad (1)$$

where $w_{ij} = (\mathbf{V}\widetilde{\mathbf{W}}_{VX})_{ij}$, and the multimodal term coefficient $\eta \geq 0$ determines to which extent the model reflects the visual information. Considering a scale constraint, Eq. (1) can be reformulated as follows:

We first define some matrices

$$\mathbf{X} = \begin{pmatrix} \mathbf{V} & \mathbf{O} & \mathbf{O} \\ \mathbf{O} & \mathbf{C} & \mathbf{O} \\ \mathbf{O} & \mathbf{O} & \mathbf{X}_{vis} \end{pmatrix}, \mathbf{W} = \begin{pmatrix} \mathbf{O} & \mathbf{I}_T & \mathbf{W}_{VX} \\ \mathbf{I}_T & \mathbf{O} & \mathbf{O} \\ \mathbf{W}_{VX}^\top & \mathbf{O} & \mathbf{O} \end{pmatrix},$$

$$\mathbf{M} = \mathrm{diag}(\mathbf{W}\mathbf{1}), \mathbf{A}^\top = (\mathbf{A}_V^\top, \mathbf{A}_C^\top, \mathbf{A}_{vis}^\top), \mathbf{W}_{VX} = (\eta w_{ij}),$$

then the optimization problem of Eq. (1) can be written as

$$\max_{\mathbf{A}} \mathrm{Tr}\left(\mathbf{A}^\top\mathbf{X}^\top\mathbf{W}\mathbf{X}\mathbf{A}\right)$$

$$\text{subject to } \mathbf{A}^\top\mathbf{X}^\top\mathbf{M}\mathbf{X}\mathbf{A} = \mathbf{I}_K. \quad (2)$$

Similar to Eigenwords, we squash $\mathbf{X}^\top\mathbf{W}\mathbf{X}$ and $\mathbf{X}^\top\mathbf{M}\mathbf{X}$ in Eq. (2) by replacing them with $\mathcal{H}, \mathcal{G}$ respectively, which are defined as follows.

$$\mathcal{H} = \begin{pmatrix} \mathbf{O} & \mathcal{C}_{VC} & \eta\mathcal{C}_{VV}\widetilde{\mathbf{W}}_{VX}\mathbf{X}_{vis} \\ \mathcal{C}_{VC}^\top & \mathbf{O} & \mathbf{O} \\ \eta\mathbf{X}_{vis}^\top\widetilde{\mathbf{W}}_{VX}^\top\mathcal{C}_{VV} & \mathbf{O} & \mathbf{O} \end{pmatrix},$$

$$\mathcal{G} = \begin{pmatrix} \mathcal{G}_{VV} & \mathbf{O} & \mathbf{O} \\ \mathbf{O} & \mathcal{C}_{CC} & \mathbf{O} \\ \mathbf{O} & \mathbf{O} & \mathcal{G}_{vis} \end{pmatrix},$$

where $\mathrm{diag}(v)$ is a diagonal matrix aligning v as its diagonal elements, $\mathrm{sqrt}(\cdot)$ represents element-wise square root, the vectors m, n are defined as $m = \mathrm{sqrt}(\mathbf{V}^\top \mathbf{1}), n = \eta \widetilde{\mathbf{W}}_{VX} \mathbf{1}$, $\circ$ represents element-wise product, and

$$\mathcal{G}_{VV} = \mathcal{C}_{VV} + \mathrm{diag}(m \circ n),$$

$$\mathcal{G}_{vis} = \eta \mathbf{X}_{vis}^\top \mathrm{diag}(\widetilde{\mathbf{W}}_{VX}^\top m) \mathbf{X}_{vis}.$$

Consequently, our final goal here is to find an optimal linear mapping which maximizes $\mathrm{Tr}(\mathbf{A}^\top \mathcal{H} \mathbf{A})$ subject to $\mathbf{A}^\top \mathcal{G} \mathbf{A} = \mathbf{I}_K$, and this problem reduces to a generalized eigenvalue problem $\mathcal{H} a = \lambda \mathcal{G} a$. Hence, we can obtain the optimal solution as $\hat{\mathbf{A}}^\top = (\hat{\mathbf{A}}_V^\top, \hat{\mathbf{A}}_C^\top, \hat{\mathbf{A}}_{vis}^\top) = \mathcal{G}^{-1/2}(u_1, \ldots, u_K)$, where $u_1, \ldots, u_K$ are eigenvectors of $(\mathcal{G}^{-1/2})^\top \mathcal{H} \mathcal{G}^{-1/2}$ for the K largest eigenvalues. Note that we obtain the word representations as the rows of $\hat{\mathbf{A}}_V$, as well as a linear mapping from the visual space to the common multimodal space $\hat{\mathbf{A}}_{vis}$, and that when visual data $\mathbf{X}_{vis}$ is omitted from the model, Eq. (2) is equivalent to CCA, namely, the ordinary Eigenwords. There are several ways to solve a generalized eigenvalue problem. In this study, we employed a randomized method for a generalized Hermitian eigenvalue problem proposed in Saibaba et al. (2016).

Silberer and Lapata (2012) also uses CCA to obtain multimodal representations, which associates term-document matrix representing word occurrences in documents and perceptual matrix containing scores on feature norms (or attributes) like "*is_brown*", "*has_fangs*", etc. This model is not considering any recent developments in word embedding. In addition, the feature norms are expensive to obtain, and hence we cannot expect them for a large number vocabularies. Besides, images relevant to a given word are more easy to collect.

5 Experiments

5.1 Dataset

In our experiment, we used English Wikipedia corpus (2016 dump)[1], which consists of approximately 3.9 billion tokens. We first used the script provided by Mahoney[2] to clean up the original dump. Afterward, we applied word2phrase (Mikolov et al., 2013) to the original

corpus twice with a threshold value 500 to obtain multi-term phrases.

As for visual data, we downloaded images from the URLs in the NUS-WIDE image dataset (Chua et al., 2009), which also provides Flickr tags of each image. Although Flickr tags associated with each image could be very noisy and have varying abstractness, they provides a rich source of many-to-many relationships between images and words. Since we were interested in investigating if the large, but noisy web data would play a role as a helpful source for multimodal word representations, we omitted preprocessing like manually removing noisy tags or highly abstract tags.

The images were converted to 4096-dim feature vectors using the Caffe toolkit (Jia et al., 2014), together with a pre-trained[3] AlexNet model (Krizhevsky et al., 2012). These feature vectors are the output of the fc7 layer on the AlexNet. We randomly selected 100k images for a training set.

5.2 Word Similarity Task

We compared MM-Eigenwords against Eigenwords and skip-gram model through word similarity tasks, a common evaluation method of vector word representations. In our experiments, we used MEN (Bruni et al., 2014), SimLex (Hill et al., 2015), and another semantic similarity (Silberer and Lapata, 2014) denoted as SemSim, which provide 3000, 999, and 7576 word pairs respectively. These datasets provide manually scored word similarities, and the last one also provides visual similarity scores of word pairs denoted as VisSim. As for model-generated word vectors, the semantic similarity between two word vectors was measured by cosine similarity, and we quantitatively evaluated each embedding method by calculating Spearman correlation between model-based and human annotated scores.

5.3 Concept-to-Image Search

We also evaluated the accuracy of concept-to-image search to investigate the extent to which our multimodal word representations reflect visual information. In this experiment, we used 81 manually annotated concepts provided in NUS-WIDE dataset as queries. In addition, we randomly selected 10k images which are absent during the training phase as test-images and used $\hat{\mathbf{A}}_{vis}$ to

[1]https://dumps.wikimedia.org/enwiki/
[2]http://mattmahoney.net/dc/textdata.html
[3]https://github.com/BVLC/caffe/tree/master/models/

Method	η	Word Simliarity Task				Concept-to-Image Search		
		MEN	SimLex	SemSim	VisSim	P@1	P@5	P@10
Skip-gram		0.77	0.40	0.67	0.54			
Eigenwords		0.75	**0.45**	0.68	**0.58**			
MM-Eigewords	0.01	0.77	0.41	0.71	0.57	0.21	0.23	0.22
MM-Eigewords	0.1	**0.78**	0.38	**0.72**	0.57	0.14	0.14	0.14
MM-Eigewords	1	0.74	0.34	**0.72**	0.57	0.12	0.14	0.14
MM-Eigewords	10^4	0.66	0.21	0.37	0.34	0.44	0.39	0.37
MM-Eigewords	10^6	0.61	0.20	0.29	0.29	**0.53**	**0.47**	**0.49**

Table 1: Spearman correlations between word similarities based on the word vectors and that of the human annotations, and the right part shows the accuracies of concept-to-image search evaluated by precision@k.

project them to the textual space, on which top-match images were found by cosine similarities with the query vectors. We evaluated the accuracies of image search by precision at 1, 5, and 10, averaged over all query concepts, while varying the value of the multimodal term coefficient η in Eq. (1).

6 Results

For Eigenwords and MM-Eigenwords, we set the number of word types to $V \approx 140$k, including 30k most frequent vocabularies, words in the benchmarks, and Flickr tags associated with training-images, and we set the number of power iteration to 3. As for skip-gram model, we set the subsampling threshold to 10^{-5}, number of negative examples to 5, and training iterations to 5. In addition we fixed the dimensionality of word vectors to $K = 500$, and the context window size to $h = 4$ for every methods. As mentioned in Section 1, one of the most related methods is MMSkip-gram, against which we should compare MM-Eigenwords. However, since we could not find its code nor implement it by ourselves, a comparative study with MMSkip-gram is not included in this paper.

Table 1 shows the results of the word similarity tasks. As we can see in the table, with smaller η, the performance on word-similarity tasks of MM-Eigenwords is similar to that of Eigenwords or skip-gram model, whereas poor results on the concept-to-image search task. On the other hand, larger η helps improve the performance on the concept-to-image search while sacrificing the performances on the word similarity tasks. These results implies that too strongly associated visual information can distort the semantic structure obtained from textual data. Despite some similar ex-

isting studies showed positive results with auxiliary visual features (Lazaridou et al., 2015; Kiela and Bottou, 2014; Hill et al., 2014), our results achieved less improvements in the word-similarity tasks, indicating negative transfer of learning.

However, the visual informative word vectors obtained by our method enable not only word-to-word but also word-to-image search as shown in Figure 2a, and the many-to-many relationships between images and a wide variety of tags fed to our model contributed to the plausible retrieval results with the sum of two word vectors as their queries (e.g. *"bird"* + *"flying"* $\approx$ **images of flying birds**). Moreover, the word vectors learned with our model capture multimodal linguistic regularities (Kiros et al., 2014). We show some examples of our model in Figure 2b.

7 Conclusion

In this paper, we proposed a spectral graph-based method of multimodal word embedding. Our experimental results showed that MM-Eigenwords captures both semantic and text-to-image similarities, and we found that there is a trade-off between these two similarities.

Since the framework we used can be adopted to any number of views, we could further extend our method by considering image caption datasets through employing document IDs like Oshikiri et al. (2016) in our future works.

References

Stanislaw Antol, Aishwarya Agrawal, Jiasen Lu, Margaret Mitchell, Dhruv Batra, C Lawrence Zitnick, and Devi Parikh. 2015. VQA: Visual question answering. In *ICCV*. pages 2425–2433.

Mikhail Belkin and Partha Niyogi. 2003. Laplacian eigenmaps for dimensionality reduction and data representation. *Neural computation* 15(6):1373–1396.

Elia Bruni, Nam-Khanh Tran, and Marco Baroni. 2014. Multimodal distributional semantics. *JAIR* 49(2014):1–47.

Tat-Seng Chua, Jinhui Tang, Richang Hong, Haojie Li, Zhiping Luo, and Yantao Zheng. 2009. Nus-wide: a real-world web image database from national university of singapore. In *Proceedings of the ACM international conference on image and video retrieval*. ACM, page 48.

Paramveer S Dhillon, Dean P Foster, and Lyle H Ungar. 2015. Eigenwords: Spectral word embeddings. *JMLR* 16:3035–3078.

Nathan Halko, Per-Gunnar Martinsson, and Joel A Tropp. 2011. Finding structure with randomness: Probabilistic algorithms for constructing approximate matrix decompositions. *SIAM review* 53(2):217–288.

Felix Hill, Roi Reichart, and Anna Korhonen. 2014. Multi-modal models for concrete and abstract concept meaning. *TACL* 2:285–296.

Felix Hill, Roi Reichart, and Anna Korhonen. 2015. Simlex-999: Evaluating semantic models with (genuine) similarity estimation. *Computational Linguistics* pages 665–695.

Harold Hotelling. 1936. Relations between two sets of variates. *Biometrika* 28(3/4):321–377.

Zhiwu Huang, Shiguang Shan, Haihong Zhang, Shihong Lao, and Xilin Chen. 2012. Cross-view graph embedding. In *ACCV*. Springer, pages 770–781.

Yangqing Jia, Evan Shelhamer, Jeff Donahue, Sergey Karayev, Jonathan Long, Ross Girshick, Sergio Guadarrama, and Trevor Darrell. 2014. Caffe: Convolutional architecture for fast feature embedding. In *Proceedings of the 22nd ACM international conference on Multimedia*. ACM, pages 675–678.

Jon R Kettenring. 1971. Canonical analysis of several sets of variables. *Biometrika* 58(3):433–451.

Douwe Kiela and Léon Bottou. 2014. Learning image embeddings using convolutional neural networks for improved multi-modal semantics. In *EMNLP*. pages 36–45.

Douwe Kiela, Felix Hill, Anna Korhonen, and Stephen Clark. 2014. Improving multi-modal representations using image dispersion: Why less is sometimes more. In *ACL*. pages 835–841.

Ryan Kiros, Ruslan Salakhutdinov, and Richard S Zemel. 2014. Unifying visual-semantic embeddings with multimodal neural language models. *arXiv preprint arXiv:1411.2539* .

Satwik Kottur, Ramakrishna Vedantam, José MF Moura, and Devi Parikh. 2016. Visual word2vec (vis-w2v): Learning visually grounded word embeddings using abstract scenes. In *CVPR*. pages 4985–4994.

Alex Krizhevsky, Ilya Sutskever, and Geoffrey E Hinton. 2012. Imagenet classification with deep convolutional neural networks. In *NIPS*. pages 1097–1105.

Angeliki Lazaridou, Nghia The Pham, and Marco Baroni. 2015. Combining language and vision with a multimodal skip-gram model. In *HLT-NAACL*. pages 153–163.

Rémi Lebret and Ronan Collobert. 2014. Word embeddings through hellinger pca. In *EACL*. pages 482–490.

Junhua Mao, Jiajing Xu, Kevin Jing, and Alan L Yuille. 2016. Training and evaluating multimodal word embeddings with large-scale web annotated images. In *NIPS*. pages 442–450.

Tomas Mikolov, Ilya Sutskever, Kai Chen, Greg S Corrado, and Jeff Dean. 2013. Distributed representations of words and phrases and their compositionality. In *NIPS*. pages 3111–3119.

Nozomi Nori, Danushka Bollegala, and Hisashi Kashima. 2012. Multinomial relation prediction in social data: A dimension reduction approach. In *AAAI*. pages 115–121.

Takamasa Oshikiri, Kazuki Fukui, and Hidetoshi Shimodaira. 2016. Cross-lingual word representations via spectral graph embeddings. In *ACL*. pages 493–498.

Arvind K Saibaba, Jonghyun Lee, and Peter K Kitanidis. 2016. Randomized algorithms for generalized hermitian eigenvalue problems with application to computing karhunen–loève expansion. *Numerical Linear Algebra with Applications* 23(2):314–339.

Hidetoshi Shimodaira. 2016. Cross-validation of matching correlation analysis by resampling matching weights. *Neural Networks* 75:126–140.

Carina Silberer and Mirella Lapata. 2012. Grounded models of semantic representation. In *EMNLP-CoNLL*. pages 1423–1433.

Carina Silberer and Mirella Lapata. 2014. Learning grounded meaning representations with autoencoders. In *ACL*. pages 721–732.

Fei Yan and Krystian Mikolajczyk. 2015. Deep correlation for matching images and text. In *CVPR*. pages 3441–3450.

Shuicheng Yan, Dong Xu, Benyu Zhang, Hong-Jiang Zhang, Qiang Yang, and Stephen Lin. 2007. Graph embedding and extensions: A general framework for dimensionality reduction. *TPAMI* 29(1):40–51.

Graph Methods for Multilingual FrameNets

Collin F. Baker and Michael Ellsworth
International Computer Science Institute
1947 Center St. Suite 600
Berkeley, CA 94704
`collinb,infinity@icsi.berkeley.edu`

Abstract

This paper introduces a new, graph-based view of the data of the FrameNet project, which we hope will make it easier to understand the mixture of semantic and syntactic information contained in FrameNet annotation. We show how English FrameNet and other Frame Semantic resources can be represented as sets of interconnected graphs of frames, frame elements, semantic types, and annotated instances of them in text. We display examples of the new graphical representation based on the annotations, which combine Frame Semantics and Construction Grammar, thus capturing most of the syntax and semantics of each sentence. We consider how graph theory could help researchers to make better use of FrameNet data for tasks such as automatic Frame Semantic role labeling, paraphrasing, and translation. Finally, we describe the development of FrameNet-like lexical resources for other languages in the current Multilingual FrameNet project. which seeks to discover cross-lingual alignments, both in the lexicon (for frames and lexical units within frames) and across parallel or comparable texts. We conclude with an example showing graphically the semantic and syntactic similarities and differences between parallel sentences in English and Japanese. We will release software for displaying such graphs from the current data releases.

1 Overview

In this paper, we provide a new graph-based display of FrameNet annotation, which we hope will make the complex data model of FrameNet more accessible to a variety of users. We begin with a brief introduction to the Frame Semantics and the FrameNet project and their underlying graph structures. Section 3 illustrates how annotation maps words in sentences to nodes in FrameNet, showing the struture of a sentence in the new graph representation. Sect. 4 discusses how the graph representation could help NLP developers, particularly w.r.t. automatic semantic role labeling. In Sect. 5, we introduce the Multilingual FrameNet project, and what comparisons of frame structures across languages might reveal by way of another example sentence in the new format, then discuss our conclusions and acknowledge support for our work.

2 Frame Semantics and English FrameNet

The FrameNet Project [Fillmore and Baker, 2010, Ruppenhofer et al., 2016] at the International Computer Science Institute (ICSI) is an ongoing project to produce a lexicon of English that is both human- and machine-readable, based on the theory of Frame Semantics developed by Charles Fillmore and colleagues [Fillmore, 1997] and supported by annotating corpus examples of the lexical items. Although FrameNet (FN) is a lexical resource, it is organized not around words, but rather the roughly 1,200 **semantic frames** [Fillmore, 1976]: characterizations of events, relations, states and entities which are the conceptual basis for understanding the word senses, called **lexical units (LUs)**. Frames are distinguished by the set of roles involved, known as **frame elements (FEs)**. Defining individual lexical units relative to semantic frames provides a crucial level of generalization for their meaning and use. Much of the information in FN is derived from the more than 200,000 manually annotated corpus sentences; annotators

Proceedings of TextGraphs-11: the Workshop on Graph-based Methods for Natural Language Processing, ACL 2017, pages 45–50,
Vancouver, Canada, August 3, 2017. ©2017 Association for Computational Linguistics

not only mark the target word which evokes the frame, but also those phrases which are syntactically related to the target word and express its frame elements. FN covers roughly 13,500 LUs, and provides very rich syntagmatic information about the combinatorial possibilities of each LU. Each frame averages about 10 frame elements, and the same frame can be **evoked** by words (or multiword expressions) of any part of speech.

FrameNet frames are connected by eight types of relations, including full inheritance (IS-A relation) in which all core FEs are inherited, weaker forms of inheritance (called Using and Perspective_on), and relations between statives, inchoatives, and causatives. Most frames are linked in a single large lattice (analyzed in Valverde-Albacete [2008]). The full graph is difficult to render, but can be browsed at `https://framenet.icsi.berkeley.edu/fndrupal/FrameGrapher`

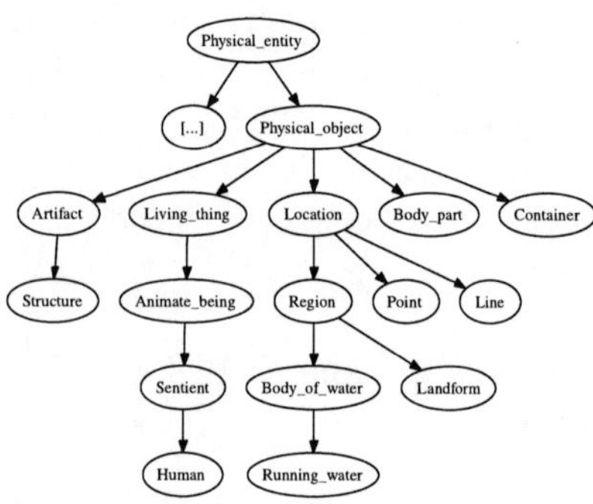

Figure 1: (Partial) FrameNet semantic type hierarchy

2.1 Semantic types and their hierarchy

FrameNet also has a small hierarchy of semantic types which can be marked on Frames, FEs and LUs; a portion is shown in Fig. 1. Many of the semantic types in FrameNet are similar to nodes in widely used ontologies, but they are limited to those which are linguistically important; for example, most agent FEs (not only those called "Agent", but all those descended from the AGENT FE in the high-level frame **Intentionally act**) have the semantic type SENTIENT (Non-sentient actants receive the FE CAUSE).[1] Some semantic

types add information which cross-cuts the frame hierarchy; e.g., POSITIVE JUDGEMENT and NEGATIVE JUDGEMENT are used to separate those LUs in the frames **Judgement, Judgement communication** and **Judgement direct address** that have positive affect from those with negative affect.

3 Frame Semantic and Construction Grammar representation of sentence meaning

The development of Frame Semantics has gone hand in hand with the development of Construction Grammar, by Fillmore and a wide range of colleagues (Michaelis [2010],Feldman et al. [2010]). FrameNet annotators not only mark which spans of the corpus sentences instantiate which Frame Elements, but also the phrase type (PT) of the constituent that covers that span[2] and the grammatical function (GF, a.k.a. grammatical relation) between that constituent and the target instance of the lexical unit as a coextensive set of spans on three annotation "layers". Additional information is added on other "layers" indicating the presence of copulas and other support verbs, the antecedents of relative clauses, etc. This syntactic information, based on Construction Grammar, can be combined with the FE labels to form a joint syntactico-semantic representation of much of the meaning of a sentence. In graph terms, the annotation process creates a mapping between the string of characters in the sentence and (1) nodes representing frame elements in the frame hierarchy and (2) nodes representing parts of constructions in the Construction Grammar hierarchy.

We illustrate this with an example sentence extracted from a TED talk entitled "Do schools kill creativity?" by Ken Robinson[3]: *The thing they were good at in school wasn't valued, or was actually stigmatized.* The graph representation derived from FrameNet annotation is shown in Fig. 2.[4]

In this figure, the nodes of the graph are syntactico-semantic entities (solid borders) or semantic entities (dotted borders) and the words of the sentence are the terminal nodes of the graph (in boxes). Each edge specifies the relationship between nodes, solid black for syntactico-semantic

---

[1] Matching FE semantic types to fillers is complicated by phenomena such as metonymy (*The White house announced today ...*) and personification (*She still runs good, but eventually she'll need new tires.*), not fully addressed in FN.

[2] Most FEs are in fact constituents.

[3] `https://www.ted.com/talks/ken_robinson_says_schools_kill_creativity?`

[4] For methods for producing such graphs, see Ellsworth and Janin [2007].

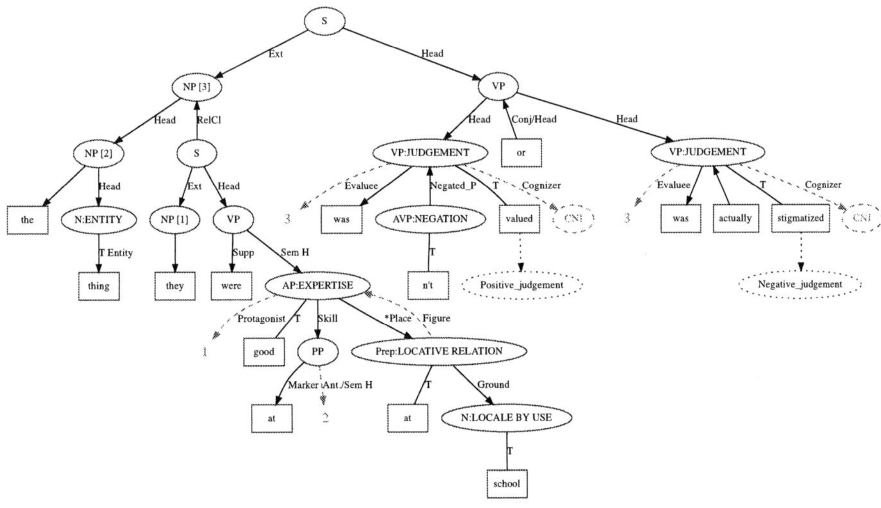

Figure 2: Graph of Frame Semantic Annotation of Example English Sentence

relations, and dashed red for purely semantic relations. The graph is organized so that higher nodes syntactically subsume lower nodes and arrows point from semantic heads to semantic subordinates. The graph is close to being a tree, like conventional constituent parses, but contains a few semantic edges that cross the syntactic edges, shown with the indexes 1, 2, and 3 (bare numbers with dashed arcs) which refer to the non-adjacent nodes NP[1], NP[2], and NP[3] respectively.

The nodes and edges have features representing the full annotation of the sentence. The large ovals represent semantics via the names of evoked frames: **Entity**, **Expertise**, **Judgement** (twice), **Locative relation Local by use**, and **Negation**. Though not shown in this graph, each frame instance is also linked to the frame hierarchy graph (Sec. 2). The edges descending from the frames semantically represent the relations described by Frame Elements in the same hierarchy. The dotted lines pointing to dotted nodes are links into the semantic type hierarchy (Sec. 2.1). The syntactic features of the non-terminal nodes are summarized by Phrase Type (PT) labels (S, N, NP, V, VP, PP, etc. with their conventional meanings) and part-of-speech (not shown). Other features on the edges are syntactico-semantic categories: T (target, the word(s) that evokes the frame), RelC (relative clause), Ant. (antecedent of relative clause), Head (syntactic and semantic head), Sem H (semantic head), and Supp (support, a syntactic head).

4 Applications of FrameNet data as a graph

The ability to separate syntactic and semantic dependency is potentially of use in many tasks involving FrameNet data, including automatic semantic role labeling (ASRL), inferencing, language generation, and cross-linguistic comparison. Because of the clear representation of syntactic and semantic dependency in the graph (displayed in Fig. 2 by vertical position, arrow direction, and non-local edges), many tasks should be able to use the graph even without special processing for the subtypes of edges, e.g. for relative clauses as seen under NP[3]. To find out the overall meaning of this sentence, one can start from the "S" node and follow the edges marked "Head" or "Sem H" to the two instances of the **Judgement** frame. From there, the application can drill further down as needed, into the frame hierarchy, the semantic type hierarchy, or the fillers of the frame roles.

One task in particular that could use the full power of such graphs is automatic semantic role labeling (ASRL). The high cost of expert semantic annotation has spurred interest in building ASRL systems. Much of this has been based on the Prop-Bank [Palmer et al., 2005] style of annotation, but work on Frame Semantic role labelers has continued, with increasing success (Das et al. [2014], Roth and Lapata [2015]). These improvements

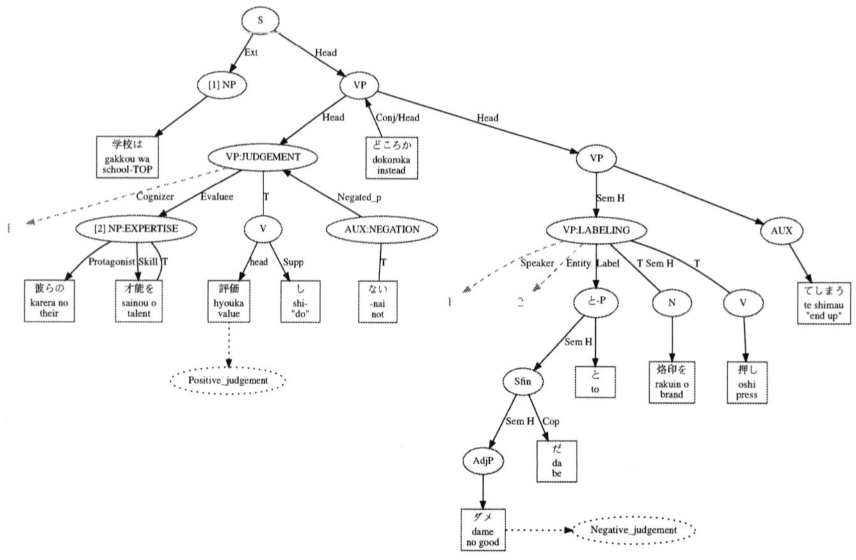

Figure 3: Frame Semantic Annotation of Equivalent Japanese Sentence

generally reflect the effort those researchers have made to understand the FrameNet data in depth, including dependencies between semantic roles within a frame, propagation of semantic types across frames, and dependencies between syntax and semantics in a specific sentence. When Frame Element annotation is treated simply as independent tags for machine learning (even if syntactic information is imported from other sources), the learning algorithms are starved of the information needed to make smarter generalizations about the large proportion of the syntactic information about each lexical unit that is predictable from other lexical units in the frame, other related frames, or structures of the language as a whole, such as passivization and relative clause structure. The current distribution format of the FrameNet data does not make this clear. Since FrameNet data is basically discrete and categorial, treating it as an interlocking set of graphs should enable better use of all the information, explicit and implicit, in FrameNet.

5 Multilingual FrameNet

The development of the FrameNet resource at ICSI has inspired the creation of a number of Frame Semantics-based projects for other languages: efforts on Spanish, German, Japanese, Chinese, Swedish, Brazilian Portuguese, and

French have all received substantial funding, primarily from their national or provincial governments. The basic research question is: to what extent are the semantic frames universal and to what extent are they language-specific? Even if equivalent frames exist in two languages, how much of the frame structure will be preserved in translation? If a different frame is used, is it a near neighbor via frame relations in one or both of the languages? These questions have also been discussed by, e.g. Boas [2009], Čulo [2013], and Čulo and de Melo [2012].

The sentence in Fig. 2 is part of an experiment in annotation of parallel texts; TED talks were chosen because translations are freely available in all of these languages. The TED talk translations are done by volunteers, so they may not be of professional quality, but this is a common situation on the web today, which NLP research has to deal with. In general the TED talk translations tend to be fairly "literal", so we would expect that the frames would be very similar across languages. However, frame differences occur even here. E.g, in the graph of the Japanese translation of this sentence (shown in Fig. 3), the first conjunct has the **Judgement** frame like the English, but the second instance of **Judgement** in English is translated by the frame **Labeling** in Japanese. Here the agent of the labeling is the school, presumably metonymic for either the faculty, the students, or both.[5] Thus, the graph representation of the FrameNet data helps to make clear which parts of the sentences to compare across languages. We hope that ultimately such comparisons will lead to graph-based MT systems that can transfer meaning at a deeper level.

One of the goals of the Multilingual FrameNet project is to quantify the patterns of frame occurrence across varied languages. The new annotation of parallel texts has just begun, so we the number of instances of frames is still small, but we can report some suggestive results based on comparing the annotation of verbs of motion in two texts. One is the TED talk, where we have annotation for English and Brazilian Portuguese; the other is a chapter of the Sherlock Holmes story "The Hound of the Baskervilles", translated by professional translators, where we compare annotation in English and Spanish. (We some annotation previously on these texts in English, Spanish, Japanese and German, but not Portuguese.)

Name Lang	Same	Partial	Diff.	Tot.
TED EN-PT	38	4	22	64
Hound EN-ES	33	3	23	59

Table 1: Frame similarity and difference across parallel texts

Table 1 gives the counts for instances of verbs of motion in two texts, showing cases where the aligned verbs are the same or different across languages. We had hypothesized that the professional, literary translations of the "Hound" text would have more cross-linguistic differences, while that the volunteer translations of the TED talks would be more often frame-preserving. The counts shown here conform to that expectation, but the differences are not conclusive.

6 Conclusion

FrameNet data is extremely rich, but not usually presented in a form that is easy for use in NLP. There are clear advantages to viewing the FrameNet annotation data as a graph that separates out entities (nodes) from relations (edges) and clarifies which information is semantic, syntactic, or both. The semantic information can be

cleanly integrated with FrameNet's already elaborate graph of frames and semantic types, while generalizations over syntactic information should enable improved use of FrameNet annotation in ASRL training and cross-linguistic comparison.

6.1 Acknowledgements

The authors would like to thank the TextGraph reviewers for their helpful suggestions. Any errors and omissions that remain are the fault of the authors.

This material is based in part upon work supported by the National Science Foundation under Grant No. 1629989. Any opinions, findings, and conclusions or recommendations expressed in this material are those of the author(s) and do not necessarily reflect the views of the National Science Foundation. The text from the TED talks was used by permission under the Creative Commons Attribution–Non Commercial–No Derivatives license.

References

Hans C. Boas. *Recent trends in multilingual computational lexicography*, pages 1–26. Mouton de Gruyter, Berlin, 2009. URL http://sites.la.utexas.edu/hcb/files/2011/02/Boas_2009e_Trends_in_Multl_Lexicography.pdf.

Dipanjan Das, Desai Chen, André F. T. Martins, Nathan Schneider, and Noah A. Smith. Frame-Semantic parsing. *Computational Linguistics*, 40 (1), 2014. URL http://www.aclweb.org/anthology/J/J14/J14-1002.pdf.

Michael Ellsworth and Adam Janin. Mutaphrase: Paraphrasing with framenet. In *Proceedings of the Workshop on Textual Entailment and Paraphrasing*, Prague, June 2007. Association for Computational Linguistics. URL http://www.aclweb.org/anthology-new/W/W07/W07-1424.pdf.

Jerome Feldman, Ellen Dodge, and John Bryant. Embodied construction grammar. In Bernd Heine and Heiko Narrog, editors, *The Oxford handbook of linguistic analysis*, pages 111–137. Oxford University Press, New York, 2010. URL https://dx.doi.org/10.1093/oxfordhb/9780199544004.013.0006.

Charles J. Fillmore. Frame semantics and the nature of language. *Annals of the New York Academy of Sciences: Conference on the Origin and Development of Language and Speech*, 280(1):20–32, 1976. URL http://dx.doi.org/10.1111/j.1749-6632.1976.tb25467.x.

---

[5]The content of the negative judgement is also made explicit in the phrase headed by *to*, literally something like "they wind up being branded as 'no good'."

Charles J. Fillmore. Valence, hierarchies, and linking. Handout for paper presented at CLP, Prague, November 1997.

Charles J. Fillmore and Collin F. Baker. A frames approach to semantic analysis. In Bernd Heine and Heiko Narrog, editors, *Oxford Handbook of Linguistic Analysis*, pages 313–341. OUP, 2010. URL https://dx.doi.org/10.1093/oxfordhb/9780199544004.013.0013.

Laura A. Michaelis. Sign-Based Construction Grammar. In Bernd Heine and Heiko Narrog, editors, *Oxford Handbook of Linguistic Analysis*, pages 139–158. OUP, 2010. URL https://dx.doi.org/10.1093/oxfordhb/9780199544004.013.0007.

Martha Palmer, Daniel Gildea, and Paul Kingsbury. The Proposition Bank: An annotated corpus of semantic roles. *Computational Linguistics*, 31(1):71–106, March 2005. URL http://aclweb.org/anthology-new/J/J05/J05-1004.pdf.

Michael Roth and Mirella Lapata. Context-aware Frame-Semantic Role Labeling. *Transactions of the Association for Computational Linguistics*, 3:449–460, 2015. ISSN 2307-387X. URL http://www.aclweb.org/anthology/Q/Q15/Q15-1032.pdf.

Josef Ruppenhofer, Michael Ellsworth, Miriam R. L. Petruck, Christopher R. Johnson, Collin F. Baker, and Jan Scheffczyk. *FrameNet II: Extended Theory and Practice*. International Computer Science Institute, Berkeley, California, 2016. URL https://framenet2.icsi.berkeley.edu/docs/r1.7/book.pdf.

Francisco J. Valverde-Albacete. Extracting frame-semantics knowledge using lattice theory. *J Logic Computation*, 18(3):361–384, June 2008. doi: 10.1093/logcom/exm069. URL http://dx.doi.org/10.1093/logcom/exm069.

Oliver Čulo and Gerard de Melo. Source-Path-Goal: Investigating the Cross-Linguistic Potential of Frame-Semantic Text Analysis. *it - Information Technology*, 54, 2012. URL https://doi.org/10.1524/itit.2012.0675.

Oliver Čulo. Constructions-and-frames analysis of translations: The interplay of syntax and semantics in translations between English and German. *Constructions and Frames*, 5(2):143–167, 2013. URL http://dx.doi.org/10.1075/cf.5.2.02cul.

Extract with Order for Coherent Multi-Document Summarization

Mir Tafseer Nayeem
University of Lethbridge
Lethbridge, AB, Canada
`mir.nayeem@uleth.ca`

Yllias Chali
University of Lethbridge
Lethbridge, AB, Canada
`chali@cs.uleth.ca`

Abstract

In this work, we aim at developing an extractive summarizer in the multi-document setting. We implement a rank based sentence selection using continuous vector representations along with key-phrases. Furthermore, we propose a model to tackle summary coherence for increasing readability. We conduct experiments on the Document Understanding Conference (DUC) 2004 datasets using ROUGE toolkit. Our experiments demonstrate that the methods bring significant improvements over the state of the art methods in terms of informativity and coherence.

1 Introduction

The task of automatic document summarization aims at finding the most relevant informations in a text and presenting them in a condensed form. A good summary should retain the most important contents of the original document or a cluster of documents, while being coherent, non-redundant and grammatically readable. There are two types of summarizations: abstractive summarization and extractive summarization. Abstractive methods, which are still a growing field are highly complex as they need extensive natural language generation to rewrite the sentences. Therefore, research community is focusing more on extractive summaries, which selects salient (important) sentences from the source document without any modification to create a summary. Summarization is classified as single-document or multi-document based upon the number of source document. The information overlap between the documents from the same topic makes the multi-document summarization more challenging than the task of summarizing single documents.

One crucial step in generating a coherent summary is to order the sentences in a logical manner to increase the readability. A wrong order of sentences convey entirely different idea to the reader of the summary and also make it difficult to understand. In a single document, summary information can be presented by preserving the sentence position in the original document. In multi-document summarization, the sentence position in the original document does not provide clue to the sentence arrangement. Hence it is a very challenging task to perform the arrangement of sentences in the summary.

2 Related Work

During a decade, several extractive approaches have been developed for automatic summary generation that implement a number of machine learning, graph-based and optimization techniques. LexRank (Erkan and Radev, 2004) and TextRank (Mihalcea and Tarau, 2004) are graph-based methods of computing sentence importance for text summarization. The RegSum system (Hong and Nenkova, 2014) employs a supervised model for predicting word importance. Treating multi-document summarization as a submodular maximization problem has proven successful by (Lin and Bilmes, 2011). Unfortunately, none of the above systems care about the coherence of the final extracted summary.

In very recent works using neural network, (Cheng and Lapata, 2016) proposed an attentional encoder-decoder and (Nallapati et al., 2017) used a simple recurrent network based sequence classifier to solve the problem of extractive summarization. However, they are limited to single document settings, where sentences are implicitly ordered according to the sentence position. (Parveen and Strube, 2015; Parveen et al., 2015)

Proceedings of TextGraphs-11: the Workshop on Graph-based Methods for Natural Language Processing, ACL 2017, pages 51–56,
Vancouver, Canada, August 3, 2017. ©2017 Association for Computational Linguistics

proposed graph-based techniques to tackle coherence, which is also limited to single document summarization. Moreover, a recent work (Wang et al., 2016) actually proposed a multi-document summarization system that combines both coherence and informativeness but this system is limited to syntactic linkages between entities.

In this paper, we implement a rank based sentence selection using continuous vector representations along with key-phrases. We also model the coherence using semantic relations between entities and sentences to increase the readability.

3 Sentence Extraction

We here successively describe each of the steps involved in the sentence extraction process such as sentence ranking, sentence clustering, and sentence selection.

3.1 Preprocessing

Our system first takes a set of related texts as input and preprocesses them which includes tokenization, Part-Of-Speech (POS) tagging, removal of stopwords and Lemmatization. We use **NLTK** toolkit[1] to preprocess each sentence to obtain a more accurate representation of the information.

3.2 Sentence Similarity

We take the pre-trained word embeddings[2] (Mikolov et al., 2013) of all the non stopwords in a sentence and take the weighted vector sum according to the term-frequency (TF) of a word(w) in a sentence(S). Where, E is the word embedding model and $idx(w)$ is the index of the word w. More formally, for a given sentence S in the document D, the weighted sum becomes,

$$S = \sum_{w \in S} TF(w, S) \cdot E[idx(w)]$$

Then we calculate cosine similarity between the sentence vectors obtained from the above equation to find the relative distance between S_i and S_j. We also calculate $NESim(S_i, S_j)$ by finding the Named Entities present in S_i and S_j using NLTK Toolkit, then calculating their overlap.

$$CosSim(S_i, S_j) = \frac{S_i \cdot S_j}{||S_i|| \, ||S_j||}$$

[1] http://www.nltk.org/
[2] https://code.google.com/archive/p/word2vec/

$$NESim(S_i, S_j) = \frac{|NE(S_i) \cap NE(S_j)|}{min(|NE(S_i)|, |NE(S_j)|)}$$

$$Sim(S_i, S_j) = \lambda \cdot NESim(S_i, S_j) + (1 - \lambda) \cdot CosSim(S_i, S_j) \quad (1)$$

The overall similarity calculation involves both $CosSim(S_i, S_j)$ and $NESim(S_i, S_j)$ where, $0 \leq \lambda \leq 1$ decides the relative contributions of them to the overall similarity computation. This standalone similarity function will be used in this work with different λ values to accomplish different tasks.

3.3 Sentence Ranking

In this section, we rank the sentences by applying TextRank algorithm (Mihalcea and Tarau, 2004) which involves constructing an undirected graph where sentences are vertices, and weighted edges are formed connecting sentences by a similarity metric. TextRank determines the similarity based on the lexical overlap between two sentences. However, this algorithm has a serious drawback: If two sentences are talking about the same topic without using any overlapped words, there will be no edge between them. Instead, we use the continuous skip-gram model introduced by (Mikolov et al., 2013) to measure the semantic similarity along with the entity overlap. We use the similarity function described in Equation (1) by setting $\lambda = 0.3$.

After we have our graph, we can run the main algorithm on it. This involves initializing a score of 1 for each vertex, and repeatedly applying the TextRank update rule until convergence. The update rule is:

$$Rank(S_i) = (1 - d) + d *$$
$$\sum_{S_j \in N(S_i)} \frac{Sim(S_i, S_j)}{\sum_{S_k \in N(S_j)} Sim(S_j, S_k)} Rank(S_j)$$

Where, $Rank(S_i)$ indicates the importance score assigned to sentence S_i. $N(S_i)$ is the set of neighboring sentences of S_i, and $0 \leq d \leq 1$ is a dampening factor, which the literature suggests its setting to 0.85. After reaching convergence, we extract the sentences along with TextRank scores.

3.4 Sentence Clustering

The sentence clustering step allows us to group similar sentences. We use a hierarchical agglomerative clustering (Murtagh and Legendre, 2014) with a complete linkage criteria. This method proceeds incrementally, starting with each sentence considered as a cluster, and merging the pair of similar clusters after each step using bottom up approach. The complete linkage criteria determines the metric used for the merge strategy. In computing the clusters, we use the similarity function described in Equation (1) with $\lambda = 0.4$. We set a similarity threshold ($\tau = 0.5$) to stop the clustering process. If we cannot find any cluster pair with a similarity above the threshold, the process stops, and the clusters are released. The clusters may be small, but are highly coherent as each sentence they contain must be similar to every other sentence in the same cluster.

This sentence clustering step is very important due to two main reasons, (1) Selecting at most one sentence from each cluster of related sentences will decrease redundancy from the summary side (2) Selecting sentences from the diverse set of clusters will increase the information coverage from the document side as well.

3.5 Sentence Selection

In this work, we use the concept-based ILP framework introduced in (Gillick and Favre, 2009) with some suitable changes to select the best subset of sentences. This approach aims to extract sentences that cover as many important concepts as possible, while ensuring the summary length is within a given budgeted constraint. Unlike (Gillick and Favre, 2009) which uses bigrams as concepts, we use keyphrases as concepts. Keyphrases are the words or phrases that represent the main topics of a document. Sentences containing the most relevant keyphrases are important for the summary generation. We extracted the keyphrases from the document cluster using RAKE[3] (Rose et al., 2010). We assign a weight to each keyphrase using the score returned by RAKE.

Let w_i be the weight of keyphrase i and k_i a binary variable that indicates the presence of keyphrase i in the extracted sentences. Let l_j be the number of words in sentence j, s_j a binary variable that indicates the presence of sentence j in the extracted sentence set and L the length limit

---

[3]https://github.com/aneesha/RAKE

for the set. Let Occ_{ij} indicate the occurrence of keyphrase i in sentence j, the ILP formulation is,

$$Maximize : (\sum_i w_i k_i + \sum_j Rank(S_j) \cdot s_j) \quad (2)$$

$$Subject\ to : \sum_j l_j s_j \leq L \quad (3)$$

$$s_j Occ_{ij} \leq k_i, \quad \forall i, j \quad (4)$$

$$\sum_j s_j Occ_{ij} \geq k_i, \quad \forall i \quad (5)$$

$$\sum_{j \in g_c} s_j \leq 1, \quad \forall g_c \quad (6)$$

$$k_i \in \{0, 1\} \quad \forall i \quad (7)$$

$$s_j \in \{0, 1\} \quad \forall j \quad (8)$$

We try to maximize the weight of the keyphrases (2) in the extracted sentences, while avoiding repetition of those keyphrases (4, 5) and staying under the maximum number of words allowed for the sentence extraction (3).

In addition to (Gillick and Favre, 2009), we put some extra features like maximizing the sentence rank scores returned from the sentence ranking section. In order to ensure only one sentence per cluster in the extracted sentences we add an extra constraint (6). In this process, we extract the optimal combination of sentences that maximize informativity while minimizing redundancy (Figure 1 illustrates our sentence extraction process in brief).

4 Sentence Ordering

Classic reordering approaches include inferring order from weighted sentence graph (Barzilay et al., 2002), or perform a chronological ordering algorithm (Cohen et al., 1999) that sorts sentences based on timestamp and position.

We here propose a simple greedy approach to sentence ordering in multi-document settings. Our assumption is that a good sentence order implies the similarity between all adjacent sentences since word repetition (more specifically, named entity repetition) is one of the formal sign of text coherence (Barzilay et al., 2002). We define coherence of document D which consists of sentences from

System	Models	R-1	R-2	R-SU4	Coherence
Baseline	LexRank	35.95	7.47	12.48	0.39
	GreedyKL	37.98	8.53	13.25	0.46
State-of-the-art	Submodular	39.18	9.35	**14.22**	0.51
	ICSISumm	38.41	9.78	13.31	0.44
Proposed System	ILPRankSumm	**39.45**	**10.12**	14.09	**0.68**

Table 1: Results on DUC 2004 (Task-2) for the baseline, state-of-the-art and our system.

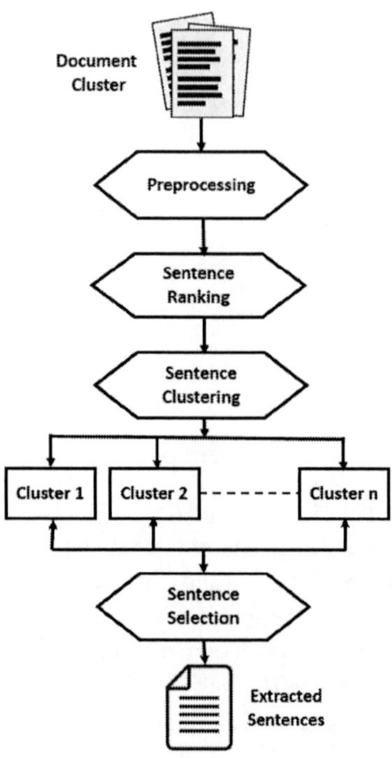

Figure 1: Sentence Extraction Process

S_1 to S_n in the following equation. For calculating $Sim(S_i, S_{i+1})$, we use the similarity function described in equation (1) with $\lambda = 0.5$, giving the named entities a little more preference.

$$Coherence(D) = \frac{\sum_{i=1}^{n-1} Sim(S_i, S_{i+1})}{n - 1}$$

We propose a greedy algorithm for placing a sentence in a document based on the coherence score we discussed above[4]. At the beginning, we randomly select a sentence from the extracted sentences without any position information and place the sentence in the ordered set D. We then incrementally add each extracted sentences to the document set D using Algorithm (1) to get the final order of summary sentences.

Algorithm 1: Place a sentence to a document

Procedure SentencePositioning(D, S_n)

  Data: Input document D which is assumed sorted. New sentence S_n which we will place in the document D.

  Result: Return new document D_n after placing the sentence S_n.

  $t \leftarrow 1$;

  $Coh_{max} \leftarrow 0$;

  $D_{tmp} \leftarrow D$;

  $l \leftarrow DocLength(D)$;

  while $t \leq l + 1$ **do**

    $\Rightarrow$ *Place the S_n in t^{th} position of D_{tmp}* ;

    $Coh_{tmp} \leftarrow Coherence(D_{tmp})$;

    if $Coh_{tmp} > Coh_{max}$ **then**

      $D_n \leftarrow D_{tmp}$;

      $Coh_{max} \leftarrow Coh_{tmp}$;

      $\Rightarrow$ *Remove S_n from the tth position of the document D_{tmp}* ;

    end

    $t \leftarrow t + 1$;

  end

  return D_n;

---

5 Evaluation

We evaluate our system **ILPRankSumm (ILP** based sentence selection with Text**Rank** for Extractive **Summ**arization) using **ROUGE**[5] (Lin, 2004) on DUC 2004 (Task-2, Length limit(L) = 100 words). However, ROUGE scores are biased towards lexical overlap at surface level and insensitive to summary coherence. Moreover, sophisticated coherence evaluation metrics are seldom adopted for summarization thus many of the previous systems used human evaluation for measuring readability. For this reason, we evaluate our summary coherence using (Lapata and Barzilay, 2005) (Barzilay and Lapata, 2008) which defines coherence probabilities for an ordered set of sentences.

5.1 Baseline Systems

We compare our system with baseline (LexRank, GreedyKL) and state of the art systems (Submodular, ICSISumm). **LexRank**(Erkan and Radev, 2004) represents input texts as graph where nodes

---

[4]Note that, we didn't take any position information of the original sentences to be extracted from the document.

[5]ROUGE-1.5.5 with options: -n 2 -m -u -c 95 -x -r 1000 -f A -p 0.5 -t 0

are the sentences and the edges are formed between two sentences if the cosine similarity is above a certain threshold. Sentence importance is calculated by running the PageRank algorithm on the graph. **GreedyKL** (Haghighi and Vanderwende, 2009) iteratively selects the next sentence for the summary that will minimize the KL divergence between the estimated word distributions. (Lin and Bilmes, 2011) treat the document summarization problem as maximizing a **Submodular** function under a budget constraint. They achieved a near-optimal information coverage and non-redundancy using a modified greedy algorithm. On the other hand, **ICSISumm** (Gillick and Favre, 2009) employs a global linear optimization framework, finding the globally optimal summary rather than choosing sentences according to their importance in a greedy fashion.

The summaries generated by the baselines and the state-of-the-art extractive summarizers on the DUC 2004 dataset were collected from (Hong et al., 2014).

5.2 Results

Our results include R-1, R-2, and R-SU4, which counts matches in unigrams, bigrams, and skip-bigrams respectively. The skip-bigrams allow four words in between. According to Table 1, R-1, R-2 scores obtained by our system outperform all the baselines and state of the art systems on DUC 2004 datasets. One of the main reasons of getting the improved R-1 and R-2 score is the use of keyphrases. Moreover, there is no significant difference between our proposed system and submodular in case of R-SU4. We also get better coherence probability because of our sentence ordering technique. The system's output for a randomly selected document set (e.g. d30015t) from DUC 2004 is shown in Table 2.

5.3 Limitations

One of the essential properties of the text summarization systems is the ability to generate a summary with a fixed length (DUC 2004, Task-2: Length limit = 100 words). According to (Hong et al., 2014) all the summarizer from the previous research either truncated the summary to 100th word, or removed the last sentence from the summary set. In this paper, we follow the second one to produce grammatical summary. However, the first one produces a certain ungrammatical sentence, later one can lose a lot of information in

Summary Generated (After Sentence Extraction)
But U.S. special envoy Richard Holbrooke said the situation in the southern Serbian province was as bad now as two weeks ago. A Western diplomat said up to 120 Yugoslav army armored vehicles, including tanks, have been pulled out. On Sunday,Milosevic met with Russian Foreign Minister Igor Ivanov and Defense Minister Igor Sergeyev, Serbian President Milan Milutinovic and Yugoslavia's top defense officials. To avoid such an attack, Yugoslavia must end the hostilities, withdraw army and security forces, take urgent measures to overcome the humanitarian crisis, ensure that refugees can return home and take part in peace talks, he said.
Summary Generated (After Sentence Ordering)
On Sunday, Milosevic met with Russian Foreign Minister Igor Ivanov and Defense Minister Igor Sergeyev, Serbian President Milan Milutinovic and Yugoslavia's top defense officials. But U.S. special envoy Richard Holbrooke said the situation in the southern Serbian province was as bad now as two weeks ago. A Western diplomat said up to 120 Yugoslav army armored vehicles, including tanks, have been pulled out. To avoid such an attack, Yugoslavia must end the hostilities, withdraw army and security forces, take urgent measures to overcome the humanitarian crisis, ensure that refugees can return home and take part in peace talks, he said.

Table 2: System's output (100 words) for the document set **d30015t** from DUC 2004.

the worst case, if the sentences are long. We more focus on the grammaticality of the final summary.

6 Conclusion and Future Work

In this work, we implemented an ILP based sentence selection along with TextRank scores and key phrases for extractive multi-document summarization. We further model the coherence to increase the readability of the generated summary. Evaluation results strongly indicate the benefits of using continuous word vector representations in all the steps involved in the overall system. In future, we will focus on jointly extracting the sentences to maximize informativity and readability while minimizing redundancy using the same ILP model. Moreover, we will also try to propose a solution for the length limit problem.

Acknowledgments

We would like to thank the anonymous reviewers for their useful comments. The research reported in this paper was conducted at the University of Lethbridge and supported by the Natural Sciences and Engineering Research Council (NSERC) of Canada discovery grant and the University of Lethbridge.

References

Regina Barzilay, Noemie Elhadad, and Kathleen R. McKeown. 2002. Inferring strategies for sentence ordering in multidocument news summarization. *J. Artif. Int. Res.* 17(1):35–55.

Regina Barzilay and Mirella Lapata. 2008. Modeling local coherence: An entity-based approach. *Comput. Linguist.* 34(1):1–34.

Jianpeng Cheng and Mirella Lapata. 2016. Neural summarization by extracting sentences and words. In *Proceedings of the 54th Annual Meeting of the Association for Computational Linguistics (Volume 1: Long Papers)*. Association for Computational Linguistics, Berlin, Germany, pages 484–494.

William W. Cohen, Robert E. Schapire, and Yoram Singer. 1999. Learning to order things. *J. Artif. Int. Res.* 10(1):243–270.

Günes Erkan and Dragomir R. Radev. 2004. Lexrank: Graph-based lexical centrality as salience in text summarization. *J. Artif. Int. Res.* 22(1):457–479.

Dan Gillick and Benoit Favre. 2009. A scalable global model for summarization. In *Proceedings of the Workshop on Integer Linear Programming for Natural Langauge Processing*. Association for Computational Linguistics, Stroudsburg, PA, USA, ILP '09, pages 10–18.

Aria Haghighi and Lucy Vanderwende. 2009. Exploring content models for multi-document summarization. In *Proceedings of Human Language Technologies: The 2009 Annual Conference of the North American Chapter of the Association for Computational Linguistics*. Association for Computational Linguistics, Stroudsburg, PA, USA, NAACL '09, pages 362–370.

Kai Hong, John Conroy, Benoit Favre, Alex Kulesza, Hui Lin, and Ani Nenkova. 2014. A repository of state of the art and competitive baseline summaries for generic news summarization. In *Proceedings of the Ninth International Conference on Language Resources and Evaluation (LREC'14)*. European Language Resources Association (ELRA), Reykjavik, Iceland, pages 1608–1616. ACL Anthology Identifier: L14-1070.

Kai Hong and Ani Nenkova. 2014. Improving the estimation of word importance for news multi-document summarization. In *Proceedings of the 14th Conference of the European Chapter of the Association for Computational Linguistics*. Association for Computational Linguistics, Gothenburg, Sweden, pages 712–721.

Mirella Lapata and Regina Barzilay. 2005. Automatic evaluation of text coherence: Models and representations. In *Proceedings of the 19th International Joint Conference on Artificial Intelligence*. Morgan Kaufmann Publishers Inc., San Francisco, CA, USA, IJCAI'05, pages 1085–1090.

Chin-Yew Lin. 2004. Rouge: A package for automatic evaluation of summaries. In Stan Szpakowicz Marie-Francine Moens, editor, *Text Summarization Branches Out: Proceedings of the ACL-04 Workshop*. Association for Computational Linguistics, Barcelona, Spain, pages 74–81.

Hui Lin and Jeff Bilmes. 2011. A class of submodular functions for document summarization. In *Proceedings of the 49th Annual Meeting of the Association for Computational Linguistics: Human Language Technologies - Volume 1*. Association for Computational Linguistics, Stroudsburg, PA, USA, HLT '11, pages 510–520.

Rada Mihalcea and Paul Tarau. 2004. Textrank: Bringing order into texts. In Dekang Lin and Dekai Wu, editors, *Proceedings of EMNLP 2004*. Association for Computational Linguistics, Barcelona, Spain, pages 404–411.

Tomas Mikolov, Ilya Sutskever, Kai Chen, Greg Corrado, and Jeffrey Dean. 2013. Distributed representations of words and phrases and their compositionality. In *Proceedings of the 26th International Conference on Neural Information Processing Systems*. Curran Associates Inc., USA, NIPS'13, pages 3111–3119.

Fionn Murtagh and Pierre Legendre. 2014. Ward's hierarchical agglomerative clustering method: Which algorithms implement ward's criterion? *J. Classif.* 31(3):274–295.

Ramesh Nallapati, Feifei Zhai, and Bowen Zhou. 2017. Summarunner: A recurrent neural network based sequence model for extractive summarization of documents. In *Proceedings of the Thirty-First AAAI Conference on Artificial Intelligence, February 4-9, 2017, San Francisco, California, USA.*. pages 3075–3081.

Daraksha Parveen, Hans-Martin Ramsl, and Michael Strube. 2015. Topical coherence for graph-based extractive summarization. In *Proceedings of the 2015 Conference on Empirical Methods in Natural Language Processing*. Association for Computational Linguistics, Lisbon, Portugal, pages 1949–1954.

Daraksha Parveen and Michael Strube. 2015. Integrating importance, non-redundancy and coherence in graph-based extractive summarization. In *Proceedings of the 24th International Conference on Artificial Intelligence*. AAAI Press, IJCAI'15, pages 1298–1304.

Stuart Rose, Dave Engel, Nick Cramer, and Wendy Cowley. 2010. Automatic keyword extraction from individual documents. *Text Mining* pages 1–20.

Xun Wang, Masaaki Nishino, Tsutomu Hirao, Katsuhito Sudoh, and Masaaki Nagata. 2016. Exploring text links for coherent multi-document summarization. In *Proceedings of COLING 2016, the 26th International Conference on Computational Linguistics: Technical Papers*. The COLING 2016 Organizing Committee, Osaka, Japan, pages 213–223.

Work Hard, Play Hard: Email Classification on the Avocado and Enron Corpora

Sakhar Alkhereyf
Department of Computer Science
Columbia University
New York, U.S.A.
`sakhar@cs.columbia.edu`

Owen Rambow
Center for Computational Learning Systems
Columbia University
New York, U.S.A.
`rambow@ccls.columbia.edu`

Abstract

In this paper, we present an empirical study of email classification into two main categories "Business" and "Personal". We train on the Enron email corpus, and test on the Enron and Avocado email corpora. We show that information from the email exchange networks improves the performance of classification. We represent the email exchange networks as social networks with graph structures. For this classification task, we extract social networks features from the graphs in addition to lexical features from email content and we compare the performance of SVM and Extra-Trees classifiers using these features. Combining graph features with lexical features improves the performance on both classifiers. We also provide manually annotated sets of the Avocado and Enron email corpora as a supplementary contribution.

1 Introduction

Email has quickly become a crucial communication medium for both individuals and organizations. Kiritchenko and Matwin (2011) show that a typical user daily receives 40-50 emails. Because of its popularity, different research problems related to email classification tasks have arisen. These tasks include spam-filtering, assigning priority to messages, and foldering messages according a user-specified strategy (Klimt and Yang, 2004). In spite of the popularity of email, many classification tasks have been hampered due the lack of availability of task-related data, due to the privacy issues surrounding email. However, two large data sets are available. First, a large dataset of real emails, the Enron corpus, was made publicly available by the Federal Energy Regulatory Commission (FERC) during the legal investigation of the company's collapse. Second, in February 2015, the Linguistic Data Consortium distributed a data set of emails from an anonymous defunct information technology company referred as Avocado (Oard et al., 2015).

In this paper, we present an empirical study on email classification into two categories: Business and Personal. We train only on the Enron corpus, but test on both the Enron and Avocado corpora for this classification task in order to investigate how dependent on the training corpus the learned models are. In addition, we provide new annotated datasets based on the two corpora [1].

We manually annotated datasets based on the Enron and Avocado corpora for this classification task. We use lexical features as well as social network features extracted from the email exchange network of both Enron and Avocado. The experiments show that when the social network features combined with lexical features outperforms the lexical features alone.

We first present some related work on both the Enron and Avocado corpora (Section 2). Then in Section 3, we describe the datasets and the annotation scheme used in this paper. We discuss lexical features in Section 4, and show how to extract social network features from the email exchange in Section 5. Finally, we present some experiments with different settings (Section 6). The experiments show that adding features extracted from graphs of the email exchange to the lexical features improves the classification performance.

---

[1] `http://www.cs.columbia.edu/~sakhar/resources.html`

Proceedings of TextGraphs-11: the Workshop on Graph-based Methods for Natural Language Processing, ACL 2017, pages 57–65,
Vancouver, Canada, August 3, 2017. ©2017 Association for Computational Linguistics

2   Related Work

Since the Enron corpus has been made publicly available, many researchers have worked on the Enron corpus with different tasks. To our knowledge, the previous effort most closely related to this paper is that of Jabbari et al. (2006). They released a large set of manually annotated emails, in which they categorize a subset of more than 12,000 Enron emails into two main categories: "Business" and "Personal" and then into sub-categories "Core Business" and "Close Personal". These sub-categories represent the two main categories respectively. The "Core Business" category has more than 4,500 emails while the "Close Personal" has more than 1,800. We compare our data to their data in detail in Section 3.

Agarwal et al. (2012) released a gold standard of the Enron power hierarchy and predict the dominance relations between two employees using the degree centrality of the email exchange network. They released this gold standard of the Enron corpus with thread structure as a MongoDB database. Hardin et al. (2014) study the relation between six social network centrality measures and the hierarchal ranking of Enron employees.

Mitra and Gilbert (2013) study gossip in the Enron corpus. They use the data set in Jabbari et al. (2006) to study the proportion of gossip in business and personal emails and find that gossip appears in both personal and business emails and at all levels of the organizational hierarchy. They use an NER classifier to label person names in emails then classify emails mentioning a person not in the recipient list nor the sender as gossip.

A related task is to predict the recipient of an email. Graus et al. (2014) propose a generative model to predict the recipient of an email using the email communication graph and the email content. The model is trained on Enron and tested on Avocado. The full enterprise email exchange network is used to build the communication graph as a directed graph, as we do in Section 5. They report that the optimal performance is achieved by combining the communication graph and email content.

3   Datasets and Annotation Scheme

As a part of the work in this paper, we have used the Amazon Mechanical Turk (AMTurk) crowdsourcing platform to annotate a subset of the Enron corpus. In addition, due to license constraints, we have in-house annotated a subset of the Avocado corpus. We use these two sets as well as the dataset distributed by Jabbari et al. (2006) (which we refer to as the "Sheffield set") for the classification task in this paper.

3.1   Labeling

Unlike Jabbari et al. (2006), we are interested in maintaining the thread structure of emails (for future work). Annotators were given email threads of various lengths and asked to annotate each email in the thread and to annotate the thread as a whole. However, classifying email content into business and personal can be a subjective task. For example, if an email talks about an invitation to a picnic for the employees families, one annotator might label this email as business email with the perspective that it talks about a business-related event. On the other hand, another annotator might have a perspective that this is personal event even though it is organized by the company.

We have provided instructions for the annotators to annotate each email with one of the following labels and criteria:

1. Business: The content of the message is clearly professional (even if the language used is very friendly) and it does not contain any personal content; it should be related to the company work.

2. Somehow Business: The main purpose of the message is professional but it has some personal parts.

3. Mixed: the content of the message belongs to two or more of the categories (typically because the sender combines different content in one email).

4. Somehow Personal: The main purpose of the message is personal but it has some business-related content.

5. Personal: The content of the message is clearly personal (even if the language used is very formal) and it does not contain any professional part.

6. Cannot Determine: If the there is no enough content to determine the category.

We added some detailed instructions to deal with certain cases:

Set	Threads			Emails		
	Business	Personal	Total	Business	Personal	Total
$Enron_T$	3,101 (82.8%)	642 (17.2%)	3,743	9,145 (86.7%)	1,401 (13.3%)	10,546
$Sheffield_{all}$	NA	NA	NA	9,857 (75.7%)	3,168 (24.3%)	13,025
$Sheffield_{sub}$	NA	NA	NA	4,525 (73.7%)	1,611 (26.3%)	6,136
$Enron_{\cap A}$	NA	NA	NA	2,513 (88%)	342 (12%)	2,855 (88.6%)
$Enron_{\cap D}$	NA	NA	NA	NA	NA	367 (11.4%)
$Enron_{\cap}$	NA	NA	NA	NA	NA	3,222
$Enron_{\cup}$	NA	NA	NA	16,223 (79.7%)	4,126 (20.3%)	20,349

Table 1: Summary of the Enron datasets

- If a message is about a social event inside the company, such as celebrating a new baby of an employee, or a career promotion, it belongs to the second category ("somehow business").

- If a message is about a social event outside the company but still related to the company, such as a picnic (usually family members are invited), it belongs to the fourth category ("somehow personal").

- If a message is about a social event which is not related to the company such as a charity but company employees are encouraged to participate, it belongs to the fourth category ("somehow personal").

- If a message is too short to determine its category (or even empty), it should have the same category as the message it is responding to, or the message it is forwarding.

- If a message is ambiguous, try to read other messages in the thread to clarify.

- If a message is spam or in the rare case that the first message of a thread is very short or empty, say "cannot determine".

3.2 Annotators

In the AMTurk task (i.e. Enron), each email thread was annotated by three different turkers. The group of turkers differs from a thread to another. We first ran several batches on AMTurk in which we assigned 5 annotators to each HIT; by studying the resulting data sets, we found that 3 annotators is sufficient and less costly, and most of the data was annotated using 3 Turkers.

To determine the consensus label, we give each of the categories in the above list a numerical label between 1 and 6, with 6 being "cannot determine" and otherwise a larger number indicating that the email is more personal. First, we discard any "cannot determine" label. Therefore, if there is one or more labels other than "cannot determine" we limit voting to these labels. If all labels are "cannot determine", the result of voting is "cannot determine" too. Then, we compute the majority vote of all labels from the three turkers, in case of ties, we take the floor of the mean of ties. For instance, if the labels are $\{1, 2, 6\}$ the majority vote result is $\{1, 2\}$. The mean is 1.5 and the floor is 1. Thus, the final label is 1. There are 5,372 (50.8%) emails in which all annotators gave the same label. The number of emails for each category with consensus among all annotators as follows:

Business	4,882
Somehow Business	17
Mixed	8
Somehow Personal	438
Personal	0
Cannot Determine	27

The average standard deviation of ordinal values (i.e. 1: business, 2: Somehow Business ... etc) in Enron emails = 0.37. For computing the average of standard deviation, we exclude any "Cannot Determine" label before computing the standard deviation per email, and if the email has less than two labels other than "Cannot Determine", we exclude that email too. We do so because "Cannot Determine" has no actual ordinal value.

For the annotation of the Avocado corpus, we hired two in-house undergraduate students to annotate two overlapping subsets of the Avocado corpus, using the same instructions as we gave the Turkers. The licensing conditions for this corpus appear to prohibit using AMTurk. In case of disagreement in $Avocado_{\cup}$ (described in 3.4), we arbitrarily choose the first annotator's label for consistency, unless the first is "cannot determine", in which case we choose the second. The average standard deviation of ordinal values (i.e. 1: business, 2: Somehow Business ... etc) in Avocado emails = 0.08. Since we have only two annotators, we exclude any email labeled "Cannot Determine" by any annotator. The inter-annotator agreement in Avocado emails $\kappa = 0.58$ (Cohen's kappa). [2]

The complex labeling scheme described here will be useful for different tasks in the future. However, for the goal of this paper, we aim to group these labels into binary classes: business and personal. Therefore, we normalize the labels as follows: we group "Business" and "Somehow Business" into one category "Business", and "Personal", "Somehow Personal" and "Mixed" into one category "Personal". "Cannot Determine" remains the same.

Finally we exclude emails with labels other than "Business" or "Personal" (i.e. emails labeled as "Cannot determine"). These emails are discarded in both training and evaluation. This label is very rare; it occurs only 0.26% of the time in the Enron data, and 0.38% in the Avocado data.

3.3 Enron Datasets

The annotated emails by turkers are a subset of the Enron corpus released by Agarwal et al. (2012), which has more than 36,000 threads and 270,000 emails. We choose this version of Enron because it maintains the thread structure of emails. From this collection, we have randomly sampled total of 3,941 threads with different numbers of emails per thread (2, 3, 4, and 5). The total number of emails is 10,573. We exclude 198 threads (5%) and 27 additional emails (0.26%) labeled as "Cannot determine". The sample has 3,222 emails overlapping with the Sheffield set of Jabbari et al. (2006) (after excluding "Cannot determine" emails). We also exclude all emails in the Sheffield set that we could not match with an email in (Agarwal et al., 2012). After obtaining the final labels as described in 3.2, we got 3,743 threads and 10,546 emails labeled as either "Business" or "Personal" from the Enron corpus. Table 1 shows the summary of the Enron datasets with the following notations:

- Enron_T: The threads and emails obtained from AMTurk as in 3.2.

- Sheffield_{all}: All the Sheffield set except those that we could not match in (Agarwal et al., 2012).

---

[2]we treat classes as completely different categories when computing Cohen's kappa

- Sheffield_{sub}: A subsample of the the Sheffield set ("Business Core" and "Personal Close").

- $\text{Enron}_{\cap A}$: The intersection between Enron_T and Sheffield_{all} in which both agree in labels.

- $\text{Enron}_{\cap D}$: The intersection between Enron_T and Sheffield_{all} in which disagree in labels.

- $\text{Enron}_\cap$: The intersection between Enron_T and Sheffield_{all}.

- $\text{Enron}_\cup$: $\text{Sheffield}_{all} \cup (\text{Enron}_T - \text{Enron}_\cap)$. In case of disagreement, we use Sheffield_{all} labels.

3.4 Avocado Datasets

The Avocado Email Collection has 62,278 threads and 937,958 emails.

We have randomly sampled total of 2,000 threads and 5,339 emails from the Avocado corpus with different number of emails per thread as in Enron.

As described in Section 3.2, each annotator labeled 1,200 threads, with 400 threads in common. The first annotator has 3,197 emails, while the second has 3,207, and 1,065 emails are in common. After obtaining the final labels as described in Section 3.2, we got total of 1,976 threads and 5,280 emails labeled as either "Business" or "Personal" from the Avocado corpus. Table 2 shows the summary of the Avocado datasets with the following notations:

- Avocado_1: The threads and emails labeled by the first annotator as in 3.2.

- Avocado_2: The threads and emails labeled by the second annotator as in 3.2.

- $\text{Avocado}_{\cap A}$: The intersection between Avocado_1 and Avocado_2 in which both agree in labels.

- $\text{Avocado}_{\cap D}$: The intersection between Avocado_1 and Avocado_2 in which they disagree in labels.

- $\text{Avocado}_\cap$: The intersection between Avocado_1 and Avocado_2.

- $\text{Avocado}_\cup$: All the threads and emails labeled as in 3.2: $\text{Avocado}_1 \cup (\text{Avocado}_2 - \text{Avocado}_\cap)$. In case of disagreement, we use Avocado_1 labels.

Set	Threads			Emails		
	Business	Personal	Total	Business	Personal	Total
$Avocado_1$	1,087 (91.2%)	105 (8.8%)	1,192	2,927 (92.1%)	251 (7.9%)	3,178
$Avocado_2$	1,035 (88.1%)	140 (11.9%)	1,175	2,851 (90.5%)	298 (9.5%)	3,149
$Avocado_{\cap A}$	340 (91.6%)	31 (8.4%)	371 (94.9%)	948 (93.3%)	68 (6.7%)	1,016 (97%)
$Avocado_{\cap D}$	NA	NA	20 (5.1%)	NA	NA	31 (3%)
$Avocado_{\cap}$	NA	NA	391	NA	NA	1,047
$Avocado_{\cup}$	340 (91.7%)	31 (8.4%)	1,976	4,826 (91.4%)	454 (8.6%)	5,280

Table 2: Summary of the Avocado datasets

3.5 Train, Development and Test Sets

For the binary classification task in this paper, only emails are used as data points. We defer the classification of threads to future work. We use three datasets for the experiments, namely: $Enron_{\cup}$, $Enron_{\cap A}$, and $Avocado_{\cup}$ (described in Section 3.3 and Section 3.4). $Enron_{\cup}$ and $Enron_{\cap A}$ are divided into into train, development and test sets with 50%, 25% and 25% of the emails respectively. $Avocado_{\cup}$ is divided equally into development and test sets (since we will not train on Avocado). For the rest of this paper, we refer to the train, development and test sets by subscripts tr, dev, and tes respectively.

4 Lexical and Local Features

For the classification task, we use pre-trained GloVe embedding vectors as lexical features (Pennington et al., 2014). There are various word vector sets available online, each trained from different corpora and embedded into various dimension sizes.

We use GloVe pre-trained word vector sets such that each email is represented by a vector of a fixed number of dimensions equal to the dimensionality of GloVe word vector set. We average all word vectors in the email using the pre-trained word vectors as follows:

$$e_j = \frac{\sum_i^n f_{e_j,v_i} v_i}{\sum_i^n f_{e_j,v_i}}$$

Here, f_{e_j,v_i} is the frequency of the word corresponding to vector v_i in email e_j, v_i is the word embedding vector in GloVe set. Both the body and subjects are included in the email content.

In addition to the contextual features, we use the number of recipient and the length of the email (in words) as meta-information that can be extracted from the email locally without looking at the email exchange network.

5 Social Network Features

The email exchange network can be represented as social networks with different structures. One possible structure is to represent the email exchange network as a bipartite graph with two disjoint sets of nodes, emails and employees (i.e. email addresses) such that edges connect emails with employees, as edges between an email and employees exist if and only if their email address appears as either the sender or a recipient in that email; we refer to this structure as the email-centered network. Another structure is a graph (not necessarily bipartite) whose nodes represent employees (i.e. email addresses) and whose edges represent email communication such that and edge exists if there is a least one email has been exchanged between the two end nodes; we refer to this structure as the address-centered network. Figure 1 illustrates these two types of graphs. In both graphs we normalize multiple email addresses belonging to the same person into one email address (node).

For each corpus (i.e. Enron and Avocado), we construct directed and undirected graphs from these two networks (i.e. email-centered and address-centered). In directed graphs, each edge has a source and destination node, which shows explicitly the directionality of the email (i.e. sender and recipients), while in undirected graphs, the directionality of communication is not reflected within edges. In the case of the address-centered graph, the edge weight reflects the number of emails that have been exchanged between the two ends and the direction; in the case of the email-centered network, the weights are always 1. Different features from these types of graphs can be extracted.

We use the whole exchange network, including all labeled and unlabeled emails to build these graphs. We include features from both the sender and the recipients (either in the "to" or "cc" list). In case of the email has multiple recipients, we

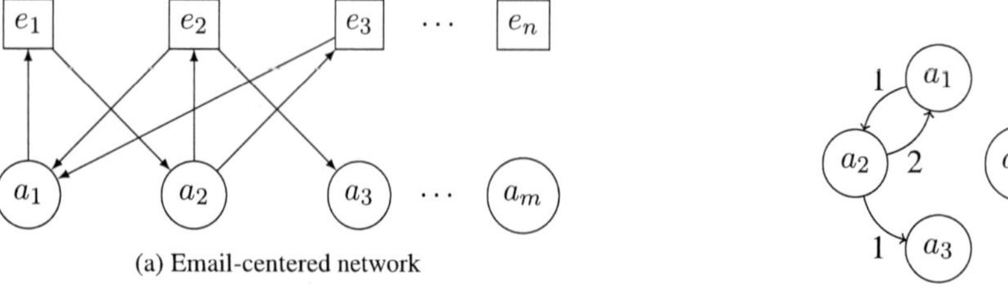

(a) Email-centered network

(b) Address-centered network

Figure 1: Email Exchange graph

Feature	Definition
In-degree[↝,†,w,u]	$indeg(v) = \sum_{u \in V} A_{u,v}$ where: $A_{u,v}$ is the weight of edge from u to v
Out-degree [↝,†,w,u]	$outdeg(v) = \sum_{u \in V} A_{v,u}$ where: Av, u is the weight of edge from v to u
Degree [↝,◇,†,w,u]	$deg(v) = indeg(v) + outdeg(v)$
# common neighbors [◇,†,u]	$\left\| \bigcup_{r \in rec} \Gamma(s) \cap \Gamma(r) \right\|$ where: rec is the list of recipients s is the sender
# Sender's triangles [◇,†,u]	$\frac{1}{2} \sum_{v \in \Gamma(s)} \left\| \Gamma(s) \cap \Gamma(v) \right\|$ where: s is the sender
Jaccard's coefficient [◇,†,u]	$\frac{\left\| \bigcup_{r \in rec} \Gamma(s) \cap \Gamma(r) \right\|}{\left\| \bigcup_{r \in rec} \Gamma(s) \cup \Gamma(r) \right\|}$ where: rec is the list of recipients s is the sender
Fraction of triangles [◇,†,u]	$\frac{2 \left\| \bigcup_{r \in rec} \Gamma(s) \cap \Gamma(r) \right\|}{\sum_{v \in \Gamma(s)} \left\| \Gamma(s) \cap \Gamma(v) \right\|}$ where: rec is the list of recipients s is the sender
In-degree centrality [↝,†,w]	$\frac{indeg(u)}{|V|-1}$
Out-degree centrality [↝,†,w]	$\frac{outdeg(u)}{|V|-1}$
Degree centrality [↝,◇,†,w,u]	$\frac{deg(u)}{|V|-1}$
Betweenness centrality [↝,◇,†,‡,w,u]	$\sum_{s,t \in V} \frac{\sigma(s,t|v)}{\sigma(s,t)}$ where: $\sigma(s,t)$ is the number of shortest paths between s and t $\sigma(s,t|v)$ is the number of these paths that pass through v
Eigenvector centrality [↝,◇,†,‡,u]	For a node v: x_v where: x is the eigenvector corresponding to the largest eigenvalue of A $Ax = \lambda x$
Closeness centrality [↝,◇,‡,w,u]	$\frac{|V|-1}{\sum_{u \in V} d(v,u)}$ where: $d(v,u)$ is the shortest-path distance between v and u.
Auth Score [↝,◇,†,‡,w,u]	The authority score for a node using HITS algorithm (Kleinberg, 1999)
Hub Score [↝,◇,†,‡,w,u]	The hub score for a node using HITS algorithm.

↝ Extracted from directed graphs.
◇ Extracted from undirected graphs.
† Features of senders/recipients in the Address-centered network.
‡ Features of emails in the Email-centered network.
w Uses edge weights.
u All edge weights are considered equal to 1.

Table 3: Social Network Features. A: the adjacency matrix for a graph (weighted or unweighted), $\Gamma(v)$: The set of neighbors of the node v

average the value corresponding to each feature. Table 3 summarizes the social network features.

6 Experiments

In this section, we present empirical results on the email classification task by conducting different

Classifier	Parameter	Parameter Space
SVM	γ	$10^{-4,-3,-2,-1,0}$
	kernel	rbf, linear
	C	$1, 10, 100, 1000$
Extra-Trees	# trees	$10, 20, 30, 50, 100, 200$
	Split Criteria	Gini, Entropy
	Min Sample	$1, 3, 10$
Both	Class-weights	{B:1, P:1}, {P:1, B:2} {P:1, B:3}, balanced

Table 4: Grid-search parameter space. B: Business, P: Personal. Balanced: class weights are adjusted inversely proportional to class frequencies in the training set

experiments on lexical and social network feature sets. We use three metrics to measure the performance, namely: accuracy score, Business F-1 score and Personal F-1 score. We are mainly interested in improving the Personal F-1 score since it is the minority class. We compare the performance of SVM classifiers and extremely randomized trees (commonly known as Extra-Trees) (Geurts et al., 2006) as implemented in the *scikit-learn* python library (Pedregosa et al., 2011). We tune the hyper-parameters using grid-search with 3-fold cross-validation on the training set. Table 4 shows the grid-search space for the two classifiers. As a preprocessing step, we apply logarithmic transformation on the network and meta-information feature values to be approximately normal in distribution. Then, all feature values (i.e. lexical, network and meta-info) are standardized to have zero-mean and unit-variance.

Vector Set	Accuracy (%)	F-1 B (%)	F-1 P (%)
BOW	92.3	95.6	71.2
6B.50d	93.0	95.9	75.7
6B.100d	93.0	95.9	75.5
6B.200d	95.0	97.1	80.0
27B.25d	94.5	96.8	80.0
27B.50d	94.3	96.7	79.2
27B.100d	95.0	97.1	80.7
27B.200d	93.7	96.3	77.6
42B.300d	**95.4**	**97.3**	**83.1**
840B.300d	95.1	97.2	80.5

Table 5: Results from different GloVe word vector sets and a BOW model as a baseline trained on $\text{Enron}_{\cap A\ tr}$ and tested on $\text{Enron}_{\cap A\ dev}$.

6.1 Obtaining Best GloVe Vector Set

First, in order to obtain the GloVe vector set that maximizes the performance, we experiment with different GloVe pre-trained vectors as lexical features (meta-information features are not included). Table 5 shows the results of classification of different GloVe pre-trained vector sets trained on $\text{Enron}_{\cap A\ tr}$ and tested on $\text{Enron}_{\cap A\ dev}$. In addition, a bag-of-words (BOW) model is shown as a baseline. In this model, we represent each email as a vector of frequencies (term counts), then we select the top 500 words using χ^2 feature selection method. In all models (i.e. GloVe vectors and BOW), we use SVM classifiers and we tune parameters using grid-search.

The results show that, in general, more training data is better, and more dimensions are better. However, the best set is the 300-dimensional 42B.300d which is trained on a large 42 billion token corpus, rather than the larger 840 B words-based embeddings. We use these embeddings in all further experiments.

6.2 Experiments with Different Features and Sets

In this subsection, we perform experiments with different models tested on $\text{Enron}_{\cup\ dev}$ and $\text{Avocado}_{\cup\ dev}$. We assume that the ultimate application of our work is a setting in which we train models on a company (i.e. Enron) and apply it to another company (i.e. Avocado).

First, we tune the hyper-parameters using grid-search with 3-fold cross-validation on $\text{Enron}_{\cup\ tr}$ and $\text{Enron}_{\cap A\ tr}$ three times: first, using network and meta-information features only, second, using lexical (embedding) features only, third, using all features.

Then, we select the best SVM and Extra-trees models with the lexical features only and the models with all features. We apply a paired t-test on the personal F-1 scores of of the models (i.e. SVM and Extra-trees models with lexical features only and with all features) using 10-fold cross-validation.

The results of the paired t-test show that the improvement obtained from adding the network features is statistically significant on $\text{Enron}_{\cup\ tr}$ ($p < 0.05$), but not on $\text{Enron}_{\cap A\ tr}$ ($p > 0.05$) using both SVM and Extra-trees classifiers.

For evaluating how well the models will perform in an intra-corpus setting, we test on $\text{Enron}_{\cup dev}$, using models trained on $\text{Enron}_{\cup tr}$ with different classifiers and feature sets. Table 6 summarizes the intra-corpus results. These results

Trained on	Classifier	features	Accuracy	Business			Personal		
				F-1	Recall	Precision	F-1	Recall	Precision
$Enron_{\cup\ tr}$	SVM	Net	83.6	89.4	87.2	91.7	64.0	70.0	58.9
		Lexical	90.2	93.8	92.4	95.1	77.7	81.9	73.9
		All *	90.0	93.5	91.1	**96.1**	**78.1**	**85.9**	71.7
	Extra-Trees	Net	87.2	92.0	92.9	91.2	68.1	65.7	70.6
		Lexical	88.9	93.1	95.3	91.0	70.5	64.2	78.3
		All	**91.3**	**94.7**	**97.1**	92.4	76.9	69.4	**86.1**

Table 6: Results of different classifiers tested on $Enron_{\cup\ dev}$. Net features include meta-information features

Trained on	Classifier	features	Accuracy	Business			Personal		
				F-1	Recall	Precision	F-1	Recall	Precision
$Enron_{\cup\ tr}$	SVM	Net	85.7	92.1	89.9	94.3	26.7	34.3	21.9
		Lexical	89.2	93.9	89.9	**98.2**	53.0	**80.1**	39.6
		All	90.2	94.5	91.7	97.5	52.6	71.6	41.5
	Extra-Trees	Net	91.1	95.3	97.6	93.1	17.5	12.4	29.8
		Lexical	92.0	95.7	94.8	96.5	52.9	58.7	48.2
		All	92.3	95.8	95.6	96.1	51.2	52.7	49.8
$Enron_{\cap A\ tr}$	SVM	Net	89.2	95.8	95.6	96.1	51.2	52.7	49.8
		Lexical	94.3	96.9	97.3	96.5	60.7	57.7	64.1
		All *	**95.0**	**97.3**	98.2	96.5	**63.0**	56.2	71.5
	Extra-Trees	Net	92.0	95.9	**99.5**	92.5	3.7	2.0	23.5
		Lexical	93.7	96.7	98.9	94.6	43.2	31.3	69.2
		All	93.8	96.7	99.0	94.6	43.2	30.8	**72.1**

Table 7: Results of different classifiers tested on $Avocado_{\cup\ dev}$. Net features include meta-information features

Trained on	Tested on	Accuracy	Business			Personal		
			F-1	Recall	Precision	F-1	Recall	Precision
$Enron_{\cup\ tr}$	$Enron_{\cup\ ts}$	91.2	94.4	92.1	96.7	79.9	87.5	73.5
$Enron_{\cap A\ tr}$	$Avocado_{\cup\ ts}$	93.5	96.4	96.9	96.0	64.7	62.1	67.7

Table 8: Applying best models on test sets. Both models are SVM classifiers trained with all features.

show that adding network features helps in retrieving more personal emails (increasing the personal recall) when using both classifiers. In addition, it is clear from the results that the network features are more effective with Extra-Trees since adding them improves all the scores.

To evaluate the cross-corpora performance, we test on $Avocado_{\cup\ dev}$ using different models trained on $Enron_{\cup\ tr}$ and $Enron_{\cap A\ tr}$. Table 7 summarizes the cross-corpora results. We use $Enron_{\cap\ Atr}$ in this experiment to test how well a model performs on another corpus when training on a dataset with few but high-confidence labels, in comparison with training on a larger dataset with labels of lesser confidence. The results show that a model trained on a large dataset with lesser confidence labels (i.e. $Enron_{\cup\ tr}$) using lexical feature alone can retrieve many personal emails, but with a poor precision. Unlike the intra-corpus setting, adding network features always increases the personal precision but decreases the personal recall. However, the best performance as measured by f-measure is achieved by combining the network and lexical features, and using SVMs, which is the same best configuration as in the intra-corpus evaluation setting. For the inter-corpora evaluation, the best result is achieved using the smaller training corpus with higher quality labels.

In both settings (i.e. intra-corpus and cross-corpora), Extra-Trees classifiers suffer in retrieving personal emails causing a decrease in the F-1 personal score in comparison with SVM classifiers.

6.3 Performance on the test set

Finally, we select the models with the highest F-1 score each both task (intra-corpus and cross-corpora), and then we test these models on $Enron_{\cup\ ts}$ and $Avocado_{\cup\ ts}$. Table 8 shows the performance of the best models on the test sets. The results show that in an intra-corpus setting, we can achieve a high personal F-1 score. Also, it is possible to get a good performance on a corpus (i.e. Avocado) when training on another one (Enron).

7 Conclusion and Future Work

In this paper, we have shown that classifying emails into business and personal can be predicted with good performance using conventional classifiers trained with pre-trained word embeddings that are available online. We performed different experiments on two corpora, Enron and Avocado. The cross-corpora results show that it is possible to classify emails of a company using models trained on another company with a good performance. In addition, we have shown that including features obtained from the graphs representing the email exchange network improves the classification performance.

We observe that the percentage of personal email decreases from 20% (in Enron) to less than 10% (in Avocado). It is not clear whether this is due to the nature of two companies or due to the spread of free email services such as Hotmail and Gmail.

In the future, we plan to experiment with adding more network features that can capture more global network features using approaches such as graph spectral analysis and graph kernels.

8 Acknowledgements

We would like to thank Ibrahim Almosallam for helpful discussions. We would like to thank the anonymous reviewers for their valuable feedback. The first author was supported by the KACST Graduate Studies program. The second author was supported for this work in part by the DARPA DEFT program. The views expressed here are those of the authors and do not reflect the official policy or position of the U.S. Department of Defense or the U.S. Government.

References

Apoorv Agarwal, Adinoyi Omuya, Aaron Harnly, and Owen Rambow. 2012. A comprehensive gold standard for the enron organizational hierarchy. In *Proceedings of the 50th Annual Meeting of the Association for Computational Linguistics: Short Papers-Volume 2*. Association for Computational Linguistics, pages 161–165.

Pierre Geurts, Damien Ernst, and Louis Wehenkel. 2006. Extremely randomized trees. *Machine learning* 63(1):3–42.

David Graus, David Van Dijk, Manos Tsagkias, Wouter Weerkamp, and Maarten De Rijke. 2014. Recipient recommendation in enterprises using communication graphs and email content. In *Proceedings of the 37th international ACM SIGIR conference on Research & development in information retrieval*. ACM, pages 1079–1082.

Johanna Hardin, Ghassan Sarkis, and PC Urc. 2014. Network analysis with the enron email corpus. *arXiv preprint arXiv:1410.2759* .

Sanaz Jabbari, Ben Allison, David Guthrie, and Louise Guthrie. 2006. Towards the Orwellian nightmare: separation of business and personal emails. In *Proceedings of the COLING/ACL on Main conference poster sessions*. Association for Computational Linguistics, pages 407–411.

Svetlana Kiritchenko and Stan Matwin. 2011. Email classification with co-training. In *Proceedings of the 2011 Conference of the Center for Advanced Studies on Collaborative Research*. IBM Corp., pages 301–312.

Jon M Kleinberg. 1999. Authoritative sources in a hyperlinked environment. *Journal of the ACM (JACM)* 46(5):604–632.

Bryan Klimt and Yiming Yang. 2004. The enron corpus: A new dataset for email classification research. In *Machine learning: ECML 2004*, Springer, pages 217–226.

Tanushree Mitra and Eric Gilbert. 2013. Analyzing gossip in workplace email. *ACM SIGWEB Newsletter Winter* 5.

Douglas Oard, William Webber, David Kirsch, and Sergey Golitsynskiy. 2015. Avocado research email collection. *Philadelphia: Linguistic Data Consortium* .

Fabian Pedregosa, Gaël Varoquaux, Alexandre Gramfort, Vincent Michel, Bertrand Thirion, Olivier Grisel, Mathieu Blondel, Peter Prettenhofer, Ron Weiss, Vincent Dubourg, et al. 2011. Scikit-learn: Machine learning in Python. *Journal of Machine Learning Research* 12(Oct):2825–2830.

Jeffrey Pennington, Richard Socher, and Christopher D. Manning. 2014. GloVe: Global vectors for word representation. In *Empirical Methods in Natural Language Processing (EMNLP)*. pages 1532–1543. http://www.aclweb.org/anthology/D14-1162.

A Graph Based Semi-Supervised Approach for Analysis of Derivational Nouns in Sanskrit

**Amrith Krishna, Pavankumar Satuluri[*], Harshavardhan Ponnada,
Muneeb Ahmed[#], Gulab Arora, Kaustubh Hiware and Pawan Goyal**
[*]School of Linguistics & Literary Studies, Chinmaya Vishwavidyapeeth CEG Campus ;
[#]Dept. of Electrical Engineering, Indian Institute of Technology BHU;
Dept. of Computer Science & Engineering, Indian Institute of Technology Kharagpur
amrith@iitkgp.ac.in

Abstract

Derivational nouns are widely used in Sanskrit corpora and is a prevalent means of productivity in the language. Currently there exists no analyser that identifies the derivational nouns. We propose a semi supervised approach for identification of derivational nouns in Sanskrit. We not only identify the derivational words, but also link them to their corresponding source words. The novelty of our work is primarily in its design of the network structure for the task. The edge weights are featurised based on the phonetic, morphological, syntactic and the semantic similarity shared between the words to be identified. We find that our model is effective for the task, even when we employ a labelled dataset which is only 5 % to that of the entire dataset.

1 Introduction

Derivational affixes are a prevalent means of vocabulary expansion used in natural languages. Derivational affixes are non meaning preserving affixes, that when applied to a word induce a new word. The affixes signify one or possibly more than one semantic senses that is passed onto the new derived word (Marchand, 1969). For example, the noun 'driver' is derived from the verb 'drive' and the adverb 'boldly' is derived from 'bold', where the derivational affixes '-er' and '-ly' are used. However, affixes that modify only the morphological or syntactic role of a word in its usage are not considered derivational, but as inflectional (Faruqui et al., 2016).

Whenever a new word comes into existence in a language, all of its derived forms are potent to be part of the language's vocabulary as well. But,

whenever a derived word is used in conversation, a human does not require an explicit knowledge about the derived word to infer its meaning. The knowledge about the source word and the affix is sufficient for her to infer the derived word's meaning. For example, if a new country is formed with name *nauratia*, an English speaker can infer the meaning for the word *nauratian* as "a person residing in nauratia", in spite of never hearing the derived word previously. Similarly, It is desirable to identify a derived word and link it to its corresponding source word computationally. It is of great practical value if we can obtain a semantic word representation for a derived word from the semantic word representation of its source word. It is often the case that corpus evidence for the source word might be abundant, but the corpus evidence for all the possible derived words need not be available readily (Cotterell and Schütze, 2017). Lazaridou et al. (2013) proposed multiple approaches, all being modifications of Compositional Distributional Semantic Model (CDSM) (Mitchell and Lapata, 2010), for obtaining the semantic word representations for a derived word by combining the representations for source word representation and the representation of the affix .

Identifying derived words from a corpus is challenging. Usage of pattern matching approaches in strings are often inept for the task. Tasks that rely on string matching approaches alone, often result in a large number of false positives. For example, while the word 'postal' is generated from 'post', the word 'canal' is not generated from 'can'. String matching approaches often result in low recall as well, due to the variations in patterns in the derived and source word pairs, even for the same affix. Both 'postal' and 'minimal' are derived using the affix 'al', but the source word for postal is 'post', while the source word for minimal is 'minimum'. Soricut and Och (2015), re-

66

Proceedings of TextGraphs-11: the Workshop on Graph-based Methods for Natural Language Processing, ACL 2017, pages 66–75,
Vancouver, Canada, August 3, 2017. ©2017 Association for Computational Linguistics

cently proposed an approach for analysis and induction of morphology in words using word embeddings. But, the authors find that their approach, though effective for inflectional affixes, has limitations with derivational affixes.

In this work, we propose an approach for analysis of derivational nouns in Sanskrit. The rules for generation of derivational nouns are well documented in the ancient grammar treatise on Sanskrit, *Aṣṭādhyāyī*. In fact, it can be observed that the grammar treatise has devoted about a 1115 of 4000 rules for dealing with derivational nouns, which is indicative of the prevalence of derivational noun usage in Sanskrit. Currently, there exists no analyser for Sanskrit that deals with the derived words. This leads to issues with large scale processing of texts in Sanskrit. The recent surge in digitising attempts of ancient manuscripts in Sanskrit, like the Digital Corpus of Sanskrit, The Sanskrit Library, GRETIL, etc. provides us with abundance of unlabeled data. But, lack of labeled data and other resources led us to development of a semi supervised approach for identification and analysis of derived words in Sanskrit. We use the Modified Adsorption algorithm (Talukdar and Crammer, 2009), a variant of the label propagation algorithm for the task. In this task, we effectively combine the diverse features ranging from rules in *Aṣṭādhyāyī*, variable length character n-grams learnt from the data using Adaptor grammar (Johnson et al., 2007) and word embeddings for the candidate words using word2vec (Mikolov et al., 2013).

The novel contributions of our task are:

1. We propose a semi-supervised framework using Modified adsorption for identification of derived words and their corresponding source words for Sanskrit.

2. We are able to scale our approach onto unlabelled data by using a small set of labelled data. We find that our model is effective even under experimental settings where we use a labelled dataset of 5 % size as that of the entire dataset. In other words, we we can label upto 20 times more data than the labeled data we have, and we perform a human evaluation to validate our claim on the unlabeled datasets.

3. By leveraging on the rules from *Aṣṭādhyāyī*, we not only find different pattern differences between the source and derived word pairs, but we also group patterns that are likely to emerge from the same affixes. Currently, given a pattern we can narrow down the possible affixes for a pair to a maximum of 4 candidates from a set of 137 possible affixes.

2 Challenges in Sanskrit Derivational Nouns

In this section, we discuss the challenges in identifying the derivational nouns computationally. The section uses some terms, which bear technical definitions as used in the lingusitic discipline of Sanskrit. Table 1, gives the definitions for all such technical terms that we use in this paper. Here, we attempt to build a semi supervised model that can identify usage of derived words in a corpus and map them to their corresponding source words. Here, we are specifically interested in the usage of secondary derivative affixes in Sanskrit, known as *Taddhita*. 'Taddhita' refers to the process of derivation of a '*prātipadika*' from a '*prātipadika*'. In Sanskrit, a '*prātipadika*' may refer to a noun or an adjective. Hence, Taddhita covers non-category changing derivations, and can be recursive as well (Bhate, 1989).

The derivation procedure proceeds by use of affixation on a word where the affix modifies the source word to form a derived word. While some affixes substantially modify the derived word from its source word, some other affixes tend to form minimal variation. In fact, the variations need not occur only at the word boundary but also at internal portions of a word. Table 2 illustrates some cases which are discussed here. In case of '*up-agu*', the derived word gets an internal change and forms '*aupagava*'. But in case of '*daṇḍa*', '*daṇḍin*' is derived, where no internal modifications occur.

In Sanskrit, there are 137 affixes used in Taddhita. The edit distance between the source and derived words due to the patterns tends to vary from 1 to 6. For example, consider the word '*rāvaṇi*' derived from '*rāvaṇa*', where the edit distance between the words is just 1. But, '*Āśvalāyana*' derived from '*aśvala*' has an edit distance of 6. Since, the possible variations that can be expected are quite high, this might lead to a large candidate space when the said patterns are used for matching the words. Additionally, a number of affixes used in *taddhita* are used for other purposes as well. For example, *kṛdanta*, nouns derived from verbs, share some of the affixes with *taddhita*. In Table 2, '*stutya*', a *kṛt*, derived from '*stu*' follows similar pattern as with the derivation

Term	Definition
prātipadika	A prātipadika is a technical term which is used to collectively address nouns and adjectives in Sanskrit. In Sanskrit, both nouns and adjectives belong to the same category
taddhita	Set of secondary derivative affixes i.e. affixes used for deriving a prātipadika from an existing prātipadika. Incidentally the prātipadikas so derived are also called as taddhita (or taddhitānta)
kṛt	Set of primary derivative affixes used for deriving a prātipadika from a verbal roots.
kṛdanta	Prātipadikas derived from verbal roots by affixing primary derivative suffixes (kṛt) are called kṛdanta.
vṛddhi	The sounds '*ā*', '*ai*' and '*au*' are designated as *vṛddhi*. In *taddhita*, it is observed that the first occurrence of a vowel in words often gets transformed to one of the *vṛddhi* vowels. This operation is also termed as *vṛddhi*.
guṇa	The sounds '*a*','*e*' and '*o*' are called as *guṇa*. Whenever the *guṇa* operation is invoked in, the mentioned vowels will be replaced in place of other vowels.

Table 1: Technical terms in Sanskrit and their definitions

of '*dākṣiṇātya*', a *taddhita* word, derived from '*dakṣiṇā*'. Now, '*kālaśa*' is derived from '*kalaśa*', where only an internal change is visible. But the similar pattern between '*karaṇa*' (Instrument) and '*kāraṇa*' (Reason) is a mere coincidence.

We can find that for deriving the word '*vainateya*' (Son of *Vinatā*) from *vinatā* (Wife of sage *Kaśyapa*, a mythological character), the '*ā*' at the end gets replaced with '*eya*', and an internal modification happens from 'i' to 'ai'. So ([$i{\to}ai$], [$ā{\to} eya$]) is a valid pattern transformation. Similarly, *gāṅgeya* (Son of the river Ganges) is formed from the word *gaṅgā* (River Ganges). The pattern ([$a{\to}ā$], [$ā{\to}eya$]) is followed. We could find more than 400 different such patterns induced by the 137 affixes.

With our knowledge from *Aṣṭādhyāyī*, we can abstract out some of the regularities in the modifications made, especially those happening at the internal portions of a word. We see those modifications as result of specific operations performed on the word. In this work, we consider two such operations, important for *taddhita* which we define now.

Vṛddhi - The sounds '*ā*', '*ai*' and '*au*' are designated as *vṛddhi*. In *taddhita*, it is observed that the first occurrence of a vowel in words often gets transformed to one of the *vṛddhi* vowels. This operation is also termed as *vṛddhi*. In Table 2, *upagu*, *pramukha*, *aśvala* and *kalaśa* are some *taddhita* words that show *vṛddhi* of its words. The operation is not exclusive to taddhita and occurs in other instances as well. *sṛ*, *kṛ* are some examples.

Guṇa - The sounds '*a*','*e*' and '*o*' are called as *guṇa*. Whenever the *guṇa* operation is invoked in *Aṣṭādhyāyī*, the mentioned vowels will be replaced in place of other vowels. In case of '*aupagava*', at a certain point of derivation, it takes the form '*au-*

pagu a', and the '*u*' gets converted to '*o*' by virtue of *guṇa*, finally resulting in *aupagava*. This operation is called *guṇa*. It is important to note that, the pattern 'ava' in the derived form instead of 'u' in the source word is result of the transformation sequence u $\to$ o $\to$ av $\to$ ava, which would not have been possible without applying the guṇa operation. For the complete derivation procedure of the derivational noun '*aupagava*' from *upagu* as prescribed in *Aṣṭādhyāyī*, please refer to *Table 1* in Krishna and Goyal (2015).

We define the character sequence which gets modified or eliminated from the source word during the derivation as 'source pattern' or '*sp*', and the character pattern that appears in the derived word is termed as 'end-pattern' or '*ep*'. The patterns contain all the other changes apart from *guṇa* and *vṛddhi*. With this knowledge, now if we look into the patterns ([$i{\to}ai$], [$ā{\to} eya$]) and ([$a{\to}ā$], [$ā{\to} eya$]), we can abstract the first component in both the pattern transformations as vṛddhi operation. For, *vinatā* and *gaṅgā* the source pattern (sp) is the phoneme '*ā*'. The end pattern for both the words is the phoneme '*eya*'. With this abstraction, we narrow down the pattern variations to about 70 end-patterns (ep). We originally had 400 patterns altogether but now we group the possible (derived word, source word) pairs based on their end-pattern only. Thus such a pair can only belong to one of the 70 possible end-patterns. Table 2 shows the end-patterns for the *taddhita* words provided in it.

3 Method

We define our task over a dataset of finite set of vocabulary C. We enumerate all the possible 70 end-patterns as mentioned in Section 2, that can be applied on a source word. With the ex-

Word	Derived Word	Type	ep
upagu (Name of a person)	aupagava (male offspring of Upagu)	Taddhita	a
śiva (Name of a Hindu god)	śaiva (male offspring of śiva)	Taddhita	a
rāvaṇa (A mythological character)	rāvaṇi (male offspring of Rāvaṇa)	Taddhita	i
tila (Sesame)	Tilya (Which is beneficial to sesame)	Taddhita	ya
pramukha (Prominent)	prāmukhya (Prominence)	Taddhita	ya
daṇḍa (Stick)	daṇḍin (One who carries stick)	Taddhita	in
sṛ (To go)	sārin (One who moves)	Kṛt	–
kṛ (To do)	kāraka (One who does)	Kṛt	–
aśva (Horse)	aśvaka (bad horse)	Taddhita	ka
aśvala (Holy priest of King Janaka)	āśvalāyana (male offspring of aśvala)	Taddhita	āyana
stu (To praise)	stutya (Worthy of praise)	Kṛt	–
dakṣiṇā (South direction)	dākṣiṇātya (Southern)	Taddhita	–
kalaśa (Pitcher)	kālaśa (related to Pitcher)	Taddhita	a
karaṇa (Instrument)	kāraṇa (Reason)	Random	–

Table 2: Derivational nouns and their corresponding source words in Sanskrit. Additionally, possible cases of false positives that follow similar patterns to derivational nouns are provided as well

tracted patterns, we identify word pairs $wp_i = (w_j, w_k) \in \mathcal{C}^2$ and represent each such pair as a tuple $t_{wp_i} = \langle w_j, w_k, sp, ep, v\d{r}ddhi = o, guṇa = p, a_{wp_{i1}}, a_{wp_{i2}}, a_{wp_{i3}} \rangle$, where $o, p \in \{0, 1\}$ and sp, ep are the source pattern in w_j and the end-pattern added to the derived word w_k respectively. The variables o, p assume the value 1 if the pattern is considered to be obtained only after the application of the corresponding operation. For each wp_i, we encode a vector $a_{wp_{i1}} \in \{0, 1\}^{|\mathcal{A}_1|}$, where $\mathcal{A}_1$ is the set of all rules in *Aṣṭādhyāyī* relevant for derivational nouns and $a_{wp_i, l} = 1$ indicates that the rule l is applicable to the word pair. Similarly, the vector $a_{wp_{i2}} \in [0, 1]^{|\mathcal{A}_2|}$ represents probability value for each of the variable length character n-grams in $\mathcal{A}_2$ learnt from Adaptor grammar (Johnson et al., 2007). $a_{wp_{i3}}$ represents a word embedding for w_j in $\mathcal{A}_3$ obtained using word2vec (Mikolov et al., 2013). For example, the word '*daṇḍin*', derived from '*daṇḍa*' can be represented as a tuple $\langle daṇḍa, daṇḍin, a, in, v\d{r}ddhi = 0, guṇa = 0, a_{wp_{i1}}, a_{wp_{i2}}, a_{wp_{i3}} \rangle$.

With the extracted pairs $W_{candidates} \subseteq \mathcal{C}^2$, we propose a binary relevance model that trains a separate classifier for every unique end-pattern.

We use Modified Adsorption (MAD) algorithm, a graph based semi-supervised approach for our task (Talukdar and Crammer, 2009). MAD fits to our requirements specifically on two aspects. Primarily the semi supervised setting helps us to use minimal set of labelled nodes as seed nodes and incorporate other unlabeled nodes into the system. The objective function penalises the results when

similar nodes are assigned with different labels. Unlike other semi-supervised algorithms (Zhu and Ghahramani, 2002; Zhou et al., 2003), MAD allows us to design the network structure explicitly as required. In MAD, every node has a label associated with it and is seen as a distribution of the labels rather than a binary assignment. The unlabeled nodes initially have no label assignments, but as the algorithm is executed, every node is updated with a distribution of the labels in the label space. The seed nodes are also allowed to be provided with a label distribution rather than hard-assigned labels. In $MAD(G, \mathcal{V}_{seed})$, the algorithm inputs a graph structure $G(V, E, W)$ and additionally a seed distribution, $\mathcal{V}_{seed}$, for the seed nodes in the vertex set, $V_{seed} \subseteq V$. The algorithm outputs a label distribution $\mathcal{V}$, for every $v \in V$.

For our setting, we find that $W_{candidates} = \mathcal{U} \cup \mathcal{S} \cup \mathcal{G}$, where $\mathcal{U}$ is the set of unlabelled nodes, $\mathcal{S}$ is the set of seed nodes used as labelled nodes for training and $\mathcal{G}$ is the set of gold nodes which is used as the test data for evaluation of the model[1]. For the system a node obtained from $\mathcal{U}$ and $\mathcal{G}$ are indistinguishable. Also, all the three sets are mutually disjoint. For every end-pattern, ep_i, we construct a classifier $MAD_i = \{MAD_{i1}(G_{i1}, \mathcal{S}_i) | MAD_{i2}(G_{i2}, \mathcal{V}_{i1}) | MAD_{i3}(G_{i3}, \mathcal{V}_{i2})\}$, where G_{ik} is a graph $G_{ik}(V_i, E_{ik}, W_{ik})$, and '|' is the pipe symbol signifying that, the output at the left of the operator is used as input to the right of the operator. Note that

---

[1] We follow the same naming conventions as Faruqui et al. (2016) wherever possible

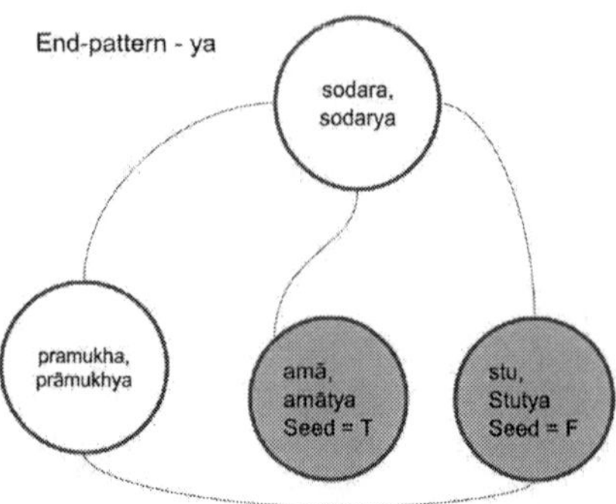

Figure 1: Graph structure for the end-pattern 'ya'. The nodes are possible candidate pairs in $W_{candidates}$. Nodes in grey denote seed nodes, where they are marked with their class label. The Nodes in white are unlabelled nodes.

the vertex set V_i remains the same for all the three graphs G_{i1}, G_{i2}, G_{i3}. Also, $\mathcal{V}_{ik}$ is the label distribution output for $MAD_{i(k)}$ and the seed label distribution for $MAD_{i(k+1)}$. Figure 1 shows the graph structure G_{ik}, for the $ep_i = ya$. Our classifier is a sequential pipeline of 3 graphs, where each graph structure uses label distribution from previous MAD run as its seed. We provide our manually labelled seed set only for the MAD run on MAD_{i1}. In MAD_i, the vertex set V_i remains same in all the runs and is essentially a set of all word pairs that follow a certain end-pattern ep_i.

In our approach, the network structure is influenced by the edge sets $\{E_{i1}, E_{i2}, E_{i3}\}$ and the corresponding weight sets $\{W_{i1}, W_{i2}, W_{i3}\}$, and both are decided by 3 different set of attributes $\mathcal{A}_1, \mathcal{A}_2, \mathcal{A}_3$ that provide the adjacency and the weights for the relation between the nodes. We explain how the edge set and weight set are defined in each of the phases.

3.1 Phase 1: *Aṣṭādhyāyī* rules

Aṣṭādhyāyī is a grammar treatise on Sanskrit with about 4000 rules, estimated to be written somewhere between fourth century BC and sixth century BC by Pāṇini. About 1115 rules of the 4000 in *Aṣṭādhyāyī*, i.e., more than 25 % of the rules, are devoted to affixation of derivational nouns. The rules related to *Taddhita* either are string rewriting rules, conditional rules, or attribute assignment rules (Krishna and Goyal, 2015). Table 3 illustrate some of the rules related to *Taddhita*, the sense they carry and effect on source word due to the affixation. We consider only the conditional rules used by Pāṇini for the task, which can further be sub-categorised as given below.

1. Phonological and phonemic - Pāṇini uses presence of certain phonological or phonemic entity in the source word as a condition for affixation. For example, the rule '*A.4.1.95 - ata iñ*', states that a lemma ending in '*a*' will be given the affix '*iñ*' when the affix is used to denote the sense of patronymy.

2. Morphological and lexical properties - Pāṇini incorporates a predefined set of lexical lists like gaṇapāṭha where words that are suitable for similar affixal treatment are grouped together. For example, the rule '*A 4.1.112*' in Table 2, states to apply the affix '*aṇ*' to all the words in the lexical list headed by '*Śiva*'.

3. Semantic and pragmatic - *Aṣṭādhyāyī* which was intended for human usage, relies on semantic and pragmatic conditions as well. We use additional lexical lists instead of the semantic and pragmatic aspects for the purpose. For example, the rule '*A.4.2.16*' applies to those words that signify 'food that is processed or prepared'. Here Pāṇini does not enumerate list of such foods, but just mentions the quality.

In Phase 1 we consider all the rules that deal with any of the phonological, phonemic, morphological and some of the semantic properties. We do not consider the pragmatic conditional rules. Each rule is considered a separate attribute at Phase 1 and the collection is represented as $\mathcal{A}_1$. We define the vertex score $\wp_k$, for $v_k \in V_i$ with the tuple t_k, the weight set W_{i1} and edge set E_{i1} as follows.

$$\wp_k = \sum_{l=1}^{|\mathcal{A}_1|} a_{k_1,l} \qquad (1)$$

$$W_{i1}^{v_k,v_j} = \frac{\sum_{l=1}^{|\mathcal{A}_1|} a_{k_1,l} \cdot a_{j_1,l}}{max(\wp_k, \wp_j)} \qquad (2)$$

$$E_{i1}^{v_k,v_j} = \begin{cases} 1 & W_{i1}^{v_k,v_j} > 0 \\ 0 & W_{i1}^{v_k,v_j} = 0 \end{cases} \qquad (3)$$

In Equation 1, $a_{k_1,l}$ is a component of the vector $a_{k_1} \in \mathcal{A}_\infty$, which indicates whether the 'lth' rule in our filtered set of *Aṣṭādhyāyī* rules is applicable for the word pair represented as the node $v_k \in V_i$ and a_{k_1} is part of the tuple t_k. A source word might satisfy multiple rules and only one of the rules will emerge as the final rule that gets

70

Rule No	Rule	Semantic Relation	Source Word	Derived Word
4.1.95	ata iñ	Patronym	daśaratha	dāśarathi
4.1.112	śivādibhyo'ṇ	Patronym	śiva	śaiva
4.1.128	catakāya airak	Patronym	catakā	cātakaira
4.2.16	saṃskṛtam bhakṣāḥ	Processed	kalaśa	kālaśāḥ

Table 3: conditional rules related to selection of suitable affix for derivational nouns from *Aṣṭādhyāyī*.

applied (Scharf, 2009). Rules that carry different affixes might find the eligibility for a given pair. For example, consider the rules 'A.4.1.95' and 'A.4.1.112'. For the word '*Śiva*' both the rules apply, and both the affixes *iñ* and *aṇ* find eligibility to be applied. But, according to *Aṣṭādhyāyī*, *Śiva* will get *aṇ* (Krishna and Goyal, 2015). But, in this setting we keep all the attributes that the word qualifies to. The complete derivation history of a word needs to be examined in order to identify the exact rule that can be applied, which is a challenging task by itself.

We consider all the rules that are relevant to an end-pattern and we form an edge between two nodes, if the source words in both the nodes share at least one of the listed property.

3.2 Phase 2: Character ngrams similarity by Adaptor grammar

Pāṇini had an obligation to maintain brevity, as his grammar treatise was supposed to be memorised and recited orally by humans (Kiparsky, 1994). In *Aṣṭādhyāyī*, Pāṇini uses character sub-strings of varying lengths as conditional rules for checking the suitability of application of an affix. We examine if there are more such regularities in the form of variable length character n-grams that can be observed from the data, as brevity is not a concern for us. Also, we assume this would compensate for the loss of some of the information which Pāṇini originally encoded using pragmatic rules. In order to identify the regularities in pattern in the words, we follow a grammar framework called as Adaptor grammar (Johnson et al., 2007). Adaptor grammar is a non-parametric Bayesian approach for learning productions for a Probabilistic Context Free Grammar (PCFG). In the grammar, we provide a skeletal grammar structure, along with the non-terminals to be used in the grammar. The grammar learns the productions and the probabilities associated with each of the productions from the observed data. The productions are variable length character n-grams.

The grammar learns a distribution over trees

rooted at each of the adapted non-terminal (Zhai et al., 2014; Krishna et al., 2016). In Listing 1, 'Word' and 'Stem' are non-terminals, which are adapted. The non-terminal 'Suffix' consists of the set of various end-patterns. In this formalism, the grammar can only capture sequential aspects in the words and hence attributes like *vṛddhi* that happen at the internal of the word, non-sequential to rest of the modified pattern, need not be effectively captured in the system.

$$Word \rightarrow Stem\ Suffix$$
$$Word \rightarrow Stem$$
$$Stem \rightarrow Chars$$
$$Suffix \rightarrow a|ya|.....|Ayana$$

Listing 1: Skeletal CFG for the Adaptor grammar

The set $\mathcal{A}_2$ captures all the variable length character n-grams learnt as the productions by the grammar along with the probability score associated with the production. We form an edge between two nodes in G_{i2}, if there exists an entry in $\mathcal{A}_2$, which are present in both the nodes. We sum the probability value associated with all such character n-grams common to the pair of nodes $v_j, v_k \in V_i$, and calculate the edge score $\tau_{j,k}$. If the edge score is greater than zero, we find the sigmoid of the value so obtained to assign the weight to the edge. Equation 4 uses the Iverson bracket (Knuth, 1992) to show the conditional sum operation. The equation essentially makes sure that the probabilities associated with only those character n-grams gets summed, which is present in both the nodes. We define the edge score $\tau_{j,k}$, weight set W_{i2} and Edge set E_{i2} as follows.

$$\tau_{j,k} = \sum_{l=1}^{|\mathcal{A}_2|} a_{k_2,l}[a_{k_2,l} = a_{j_2,l}] \qquad (4)$$

$$E_{i2}^{v_k,v_j} = \begin{cases} 1 & \tau_{j,k} > 0 \\ 0 & \tau_{j,k} = 0 \end{cases} \qquad (5)$$

$$W_{i2}^{v_k,v_j} = \begin{cases} \sigma(\tau_{j,k}) & \tau_{j,k} > 0 \\ 0 & \tau_{j,k} = 0 \end{cases} \qquad (6)$$

As mentioned, we use the label distribution per

node obtained from phase 1 as the seed labels in this setting.

3.3 Phase 3: Semantic Word vectors

In phase 3, we try to leverage the similarity between word embeddings (Mikolov et al., 2013) to propagate the labels. Due to limited resources at our disposal, we find it difficult to train word embeddings for Sanskrit. We resort to finding synonyms of words using the digitised version of Monier-Williams Sanskrit-English dictionary and then use the corresponding pre-trained English word vectors for the task. We find the word vectors only for the source words as the dictionary entries for derived words are even scarcer to obtain. Since we perform only a dictionary lookup for finding the synonyms of a word, we do not get embeddings for named entities from the dictionary. A given word might have multiple senses in English and hence multiple English synonyms. In such cases, we find all possible similarity scores and take the maximum score among them.

We use cosine similarity between the word vectors as the edge weight in this phase. For each node, for which we were able to obtain a word vector, we find its cosine similarity with that of every other node in the graph for which there exists a word vector. We find that our graph structure G_{i3} for many end-patterns results in multiple disconnected components, as not all words in $W_{candidates}$ has an entry in the dictionary. We assign teleportation probability to every node in the graph in order to handle this issue.

4 Experiments

We explain the experimental settings and evaluation parameters for our model in this section.

4.1 Dataset

We use multiple lexicons and corpora to obtain our vocabulary $\mathcal{C}$. We use IndoWordNet (Kulkarni et al., 2010), the Digital Corpus of Sanskrit[2], a digitised version of the Monier Williams[3] Sanskrit-English dictionary, a digitised version of the Apte Sanskrit-Sanskrit Dictionary (Goyal et al., 2012) and we also utiilise the lexicon employed in the Sanskrit Heritage Engine (Goyal and Huet, 2016). We obtained close to 170,000 unique word lemmas from the combined resources.

---

[2]http://kjc-sv013.kjc.uni-heidelberg.de/dcs/
[3]http://www.sanskrit-lexicon.uni-koeln.de/monier/

Obtaining Ground Truth Data - For our classifier MAD, we obtain the seed labels $\mathcal{S}$ and the gold labels $\mathcal{G}$ from a digitised version of Apte Sanskrit-Sanskrit dictionary. The dictionary has preserved the etymological information of the entries in the dictionary. For each end-pattern we filtered out the pair of words which are related by *Taddhita* affixes. Seed nodes for the negative class were obtained using candidate pairs which were either marked as *kṛdanta* words in the Apte Dictionary or were found in the dictionary, but are not related to each other. Additionally, we manually tagged some word pairs so as to obtain a balanced set of labels. We narrowed to 11 separate end-patterns for which we have at least 100 candidate pairs and have at least 5 % of word pairs as seed nodes in comparison to the the the size of the candidate pairs for the end-pattern. Table 4 shows the statistics related to each of the 11 end-patterns on which we have performed our experiments.

4.2 Baselines

We propose the following systems as the competing systems. We use label propagation (Zhu and Ghahramani, 2002) as a strong baseline and we also compare the output at each of the phase as separate baseline systems. Altogether we compare four systems as follows:

1. Label Propagation (LP_i) - We propose a label propagation based semi supervised classifier (Pedregosa et al., 2011) for each of the end-pattern. For each node, we find the top K similar nodes and assign edges to only those nodes, where K is a user given parameter. The similarity is obtained from a feature vector that defines a node, with features from the first 2 phases incorporated into a single feature vector. We do not use the word embeddings from Phase 3 directly, but find the cosine similarity between the embeddings of the words and perform a weighted sum with the similarity score obtained from the similarity obtained from the combined feature vector.

2. $MADB1_i$ - We report the performance of the system $MADB1_i = \{MAD_{i1}(G_{i1}, \mathcal{S}_i)\}$, where we define the network structure only based on the Phase 1 in Section 3

3. $MADB2_i$ - We report the performance of the system $MADB2_i = \{MAD_{i1}(G_{i1}, \mathcal{S}_i)| MAD_{i2}(G_{i2}, \mathcal{V}_{i1})\}$, where we define the settings for MAD_{i1}, MAD_{i2} based on the de-

End-pattern	$W_{candidates}$	Seed $\mathcal{S}$	Gold Labels $\mathcal{G}$	Recall	Precision	Accuracy
a	2500	350	88	0.77	0.72	73.86
aka	1200	120	30	0.67	0.77	73.33
in	1656	270	68	0.82	0.74	76.47
ya	1566	258	64	0.72	0.7	70.31
i	1455	166	42	0.52	0.55	54.76
ika	803	122	30	0.6	0.69	66.67
tā	644	34	12	0.5	0.6	58.33
la	360	48	12	0.67	0.8	75
tva	303	22	12	0.67	0.8	75
iya	244	40	12	0.67	0.67	66.67
eya	181	34	12	0.83	0.71	75

Table 4: Recall (R), Precision (P) and Accuracy (A) for the candidate nodes evaluated on the gold labels.

scription in Phase 1 and Phase 2 respectively, as defined in Section 3

4. MAD_i - This is the proposed system, as defined in Section 3

4.3 Results

Table 4 shows the final results of our proposed system MAD_i, for each of the 11 end patterns. We report the Precision, Recall and Accuracy for each of the classifier w.r.t the true class. Our results are calculated based on the predictions over the test data in $\mathcal{G}$. Seven of Eleven patterns have an accuracy above 70 %. End-pattern 'i' is reported to perform the least among the 11 patterns provided. We find that the average degree for G_{i1} for the pattern 'i' is about 77.62, much higher than the macro average degree for G_{i1} for all the patterns, which is 43.86. This is primarily due to the restrictive nature of node selection that is employed for the pattern 'i' as per Aṣṭādhyāyī. We have selected only those nodes which have the *vṛddhi* attribute set to 1 and only those source words which end in 'a'. This has led to higher average degree among the nodes that got filtered as per Aṣṭādhyāyī rules. In order to keep uniform settings for all the systems, we do not deviate from the design. But, for pattern 'i',when we randomly down-sample the number of neighbours to 44 (to match with the macro average), the accuracy increases to 61.9 %.

Table 5 shows the results for the competing systems. We compare the performance of 5 end-patterns, selected based on the vertex set size V_{i1}. Our proposed system, MAD_i performs the best for all the 5 patterns. Interestingly, $MADB2_i$ is the second best-performing system in all the cases beating LP_i. For the pattern 'aka', the share of word vectors available was $< 10\%$ overall. So, in effect, only one of the false positive nodes got the true negative label, after the third step is performed. Thus the recall remains the same after

Pattern	System	P	R	A
a	MAD	0.72	0.77	73.86
	MADB2	0.68	0.68	68.18
	MADB1	0.49	0.52	48.86
	LP	0.55	0.59	55.68
aka	MAD	0.77	0.67	73.33
	MADB2	0.71	0.67	70
	MADB1	0.43	0.4	43.33
	LP	0.75	0.6	70
in	MAD	0.74	0.82	76.47
	MADB2	0.67	0.70	67.65
	MADB1	0.51	0.56	51.47
	LP	0.63	0.65	63.23
ya	MAD	0.7	0.72	70.31
	MADB2	0.61	0.62	60.94
	MADB1	0.53	0.59	53.12
	LP	0.56	0.63	56.25
i	MAD	0.55	0.52	54.76
	MADB2	0.44	0.38	45.24
	MADB1	0.3	0.29	30.95
	LP	0.37	0.33	38.09

Table 5: Comparative performance of the four competing models.

both the steps.

In Label Propagation, we experimented with the parameter K with different values, $K \in \{10, 20, 30, 40, 50, 60\}$, and found that $K = 40$, provides the best results for 3 of the 5 end-patterns. We find that for those 3 patterns ('a','in','i'), the entire vertex set has *vṛddhi* attribute set to the same value. For the other two ('ya','aka'), $K = 50$ gave the best results. Here, the vertex set has nodes where the *vṛddhi* attribute is set to either of the values. We report the best result for each of the system in Table 5.

4.4 Evaluation for Unlabeled Nodes

In order to evaluate the effectiveness of our system, we pick nodes from unlabelled set $\mathcal{U}$ and evaluate the word-pairs based on human evaluation. We take top 5 unlabeled nodes predicted as *taddhita* and top 3 unlabelled nodes predicted as not *taddhita* from each of the the 11 end-patterns. We collate the predictions and divide them into 3 lists of 22 entries each, as the remaining 22 of the original 88 were filtered out. Seven experts, with background in Sanskrit linguistics labelled the dataset, of which one of the expert evaluator is an author. We divide the set of 66 nodes into 3 mutually disjoint sets, and each set is evaluated by 3 experts. We altogether receive 9 impressions of which the author evaluator and one of the other expert evaluator performed 2 impressions each. In case of a conflict, we go with the majority votes for each of the set. Since the entries are selected from the top scoring nodes, we expected the results to be better than the macro-average performance of the system. We find that the evaluation of our system provides a precision of 0.84, recall of 0.91 and an accuracy 81.82 micro averaged over the 66 predictions.

5   Related Work

Computational analysis of derivational word forms is gaining some traction in the NLP community. Lazaridou et al. (2013) used CDSM (Mitchell and Lapata, 2010) for derivational nouns, originally designed to learn representation for phrases. Cotterell and Schütze (2017), extended the concept of CDSM for derivational word forms with neural models. The authors put forward the idea of jointly handling the segmentation of words into morphemes and semantic synthesis of the word forms to improve the performance of a system for both the tasks. Bhatia et al. (2016), does not make a distinction of inflected word-forms or derivational affixes, but their work can be employed to learn embeddings for a word-form from its morphemes.

Soricut and Och (2015) introduced an unsupervised method of inducing affixal transformations between words using word embeddings. Faruqui et al. (2016) further propose a semi supervised graph based approach for morpho-syntactic lexicon induction. The authors show the effectiveness of their model for inflectional morphology over multiple languages. In Sanskrit, Krishna and Goyal (2015) automated the derivation of Taddhita, where the authors follow an object oriented framework. Deo (2007) have preformed an in depth linguistic analysis of inheritance network used by Pāṇini in handling affixation in Taddhita.

6   Discussion

In Sanskrit, multiple affixes may give rise to similar patterns. In fact, an affix in Sanskrit contains two parts, where one part pertains to the pattern to be induced, and other is a marker which gets elided before the affixation. The presence of the marker, termed as '*it*' marker, also plays a role in determining the type of rules that get triggered during the derivation. For example, consider the word '*prāmukhya*' derived from '*pramukha*' and the word '*sodarya*' from '*sodara*'. Both the words have the same end-pattern '*ya*'. However, only in the case of the former, *vṛddhi* operation takes place but not in the latter. Now, affixes that carry the same pattern might differ by the '*it*' markers. Now, by encoding every candidate word pairs with the suitability of rules of *Aṣṭādhyāyī* in $\mathcal{A}_1$, we can narrow down the possible candidates for the affix to at most 4 candidates of the 137 possible affixes. In order to disambiguate further, we require semantic and pragmatic level information, which is currently unavailable. In this work, we only consider the derivations in *taddhita*, as we find that jointly modelling a system for both *kṛdanta* and *taddhita* is challenging. The rule arrangement for *kṛdanta* is different from that of *taddhita* in *Aṣṭādhyāyī*, thus we require a different model design for organising the rules in $\mathcal{A}_1$, i.e., the phase 1 in Section 3. Hence, in this work we restrict ourselves to resolving *taddhita* nouns, which is the larger section in *Aṣṭādhyāyī* among the two.

7   Conclusion

In this work, we developed a graph based semi supervised approach for analysis of derivative nouns in Sanskrit. We successfully integrate the rules from *Aṣṭādhyāyī*, variable length character n-grams learnt from Adaptor grammar and word embeddings to build a 3 step sequential pipeline for the task. We find that our work outperforms label propagation, which primarily shows the effect of explicit design of network structure. We find that using the label distribution outputs at each phase, for the input at the successive phases improve the results of the model. Our work will be beneficial to the Sanskrit Computational Linguistic community for analysis of derivational words in the digitised ancient manuscripts, as no other analyser in Sanskrit currently handles derivational nouns. Our work doubles as a tool for pedagogy, as we are able to abstract out regularities between the patterns and narrow down the possible affix candidates for a word pair to four.

References

Saroja Bhate. 1989. *Panini's taddhita rules.* University of Poona.

Parminder Bhatia, Robert Guthrie, and Jacob Eisenstein. 2016. Morphological priors for probabilistic neural word embeddings. In *Proceedings of the 2016 Conference on Empirical Methods in Natural Language Processing.* Association for Computational Linguistics, Austin, Texas, pages 490–500. https://aclweb.org/anthology/D16-1047.

Ryan Cotterell and Hinrich Schütze. 2017. Joint semantic synthesis and morphological analysis of the derived word. *Transactions of the Association for Computational Linguistics* .

Ashwini Deo. 2007. Derivational morphology in inheritance-based lexica: Insights from pāini. *Lingua* 117(1):175–201.

Manaal Faruqui, Ryan McDonald, and Radu Soricut. 2016. Morpho-syntactic lexicon generation using graph-based semi-supervised learning. *Transactions of the Association for Computational Linguistics* 4:1–16.

Pawan Goyal and Gérard Huet. 2016. Design and analysis of a lean interface for sanskrit corpus annotation. *Journal of Language Modelling* 4(2):145–182.

Pawan Goyal, Gérard P Huet, Amba P Kulkarni, Peter M Scharf, and Ralph Bunker. 2012. A distributed platform for sanskrit processing. In *COLING.* pages 1011–1028.

Mark Johnson, Thomas L Griffiths, Sharon Goldwater, et al. 2007. Adaptor grammars: A framework for specifying compositional nonparametric bayesian models. *Advances in neural information processing systems* 19:641.

Paul Kiparsky. 1994. Paninian linguistics. *The Encyclopedia of Language and Linguistics* 6:2918–2923.

Donald E Knuth. 1992. Two notes on notation. *The American Mathematical Monthly* 99(5):403–422.

Amrith Krishna and Pawan Goyal. 2015. Towards automating the generation of derivative nouns in sanskrit by simulating panini. *arXiv preprint arXiv:1512.05670* .

Amrith Krishna, Pavankumar Satuluri, Shubham Sharma, Apurv Kumar, and Pawan Goyal. 2016. Compound type identification in sanskrit: What roles do the corpus and grammar play? In *Proceedings of the 6th Workshop on South and Southeast Asian Natural Language Processing (WSSANLP2016).* The COLING 2016 Organizing Committee, Osaka, Japan, pages 1–10. http://aclweb.org/anthology/W16-3701.

Malhar Kulkarni, Chaitali Dangarikar, Irawati Kulkarni, Abhishek Nanda, and Pushpak Bhattacharyya. 2010. Introducing sanskrit wordnet. In *Proceedings on the 5th Global Wordnet Conference (GWC 2010), Narosa, Mumbai.* pages 287–294.

Angeliki Lazaridou, Marco Marelli, Roberto Zamparelli, and Marco Baroni. 2013. Compositional-ly derived representations of morphologically complex words in distributional semantics. In *ACL (1).* Citeseer, pages 1517–1526.

Hans Marchand. 1969. *The categories and types of present-day English word-formation: A synchronic-diachronic approach.* Beck.

Tomas Mikolov, Ilya Sutskever, Kai Chen, Greg S Corrado, and Jeff Dean. 2013. Distributed representations of words and phrases and their compositionality. In *Advances in neural information processing systems.* pages 3111–3119.

Jeff Mitchell and Mirella Lapata. 2010. Composition in distributional models of semantics. *Cognitive science* 34(8):1388–1429.

F. Pedregosa, G. Varoquaux, A. Gramfort, V. Michel, B. Thirion, O. Grisel, M. Blondel, P. Prettenhofer, R. Weiss, V. Dubourg, J. Vanderplas, A. Passos, D. Cournapeau, M. Brucher, M. Perrot, and E. Duchesnay. 2011. Scikit-learn: Machine learning in Python. *Journal of Machine Learning Research* 12:2825–2830.

P Scharf. 2009. Rule selection in the a ādhyā yi or is pāinis grammar mechanistic. In *Proceedings of the 14th World Sanskrit Conference, Kyoto University, Kyoto.*

Radu Soricut and Franz Josef Och. 2015. Unsupervised morphology induction using word embeddings. In *HLT-NAACL.* pages 1627–1637.

Partha Talukdar and Koby Crammer. 2009. New regularized algorithms for transductive learning. *Machine Learning and Knowledge Discovery in Databases* pages 442–457.

Ke Zhai, Jordan Boyd-Graber, and Shay B Cohen. 2014. Online adaptor grammars with hybrid inference. *Transactions of the Association for Computational Linguistics* 2:465–476.

Dengyong Zhou, Olivier Bousquet, Thomas Navin Lal, Jason Weston, and Bernhard Schölkopf. 2003. Learning with local and global consistency. In *NIPS.* volume 16, pages 321–328.

Xiaojin Zhu and Zoubin Ghahramani. 2002. Learning from labeled and unlabeled data with label propagation .

Evaluating text coherence based on semantic similarity graph

Jan Wira Gotama Putra and **Takenobu Tokunaga**
School of Computing
Tokyo Institute of Technology
Tokyo Meguro Ôokayama 2-12-1 152-8550, Japan
gotama.w.aa@m.titech.ac.jp   take@c.titech.ac.jp

Abstract

Coherence is a crucial feature of text because it is indispensable for conveying its communication purpose and meaning to its readers. In this paper, we propose an unsupervised text coherence scoring based on graph construction in which edges are established between semantically similar sentences represented by vertices. The sentence similarity is calculated based on the cosine similarity of semantic vectors representing sentences. We provide three graph construction methods establishing an edge from a given vertex to a preceding adjacent vertex, to a single similar vertex, or to multiple similar vertices. We evaluated our methods in the document discrimination task and the insertion task by comparing our proposed methods to the supervised (Entity Grid) and unsupervised (Entity Graph) baselines. In the document discrimination task, our method outperformed the unsupervised baseline but could not do the supervised baseline, while in the insertion task, our method outperformed both baselines.

1 Introduction

Coherence plays an important role in a text because it enables a text to convey its communication purpose and meaning to its readers (Bamberg, 1983; Grosz and Sidner, 1986). Coherence also decreases reading time as a more coherent text is easier to read with less reader's cognitive load (Todirascu et al., 2016). While there is no single agreed definition of coherence, we can compile several definitions of coherence and note its important aspects.

First, a text is coherent if it can convey its communication purpose and meaning to its readers (Wolf and Gibson, 2005; Somasundaran et al., 2014; Feng et al., 2014). Second, a text needs to be integrated as a whole, rather than a series of independent sentences (Bamberg, 1983; Garing, 2014). It means that sentences in the text are centralised around a certain theme or topic, and are arranged in a particular order in terms of logical, spatial, and temporal relations. Third, every sentence in a coherent text has relation(s) to each other (Halliday and Hasan, 1976; Grosz and Sidner, 1986; Mann and Thompson, 1988; Wolf and Gibson, 2005). It suggests that a text exhibits discourse/rhetorical relation and cohesion. Fourth, text coherence is greatly influenced by the presence of a certain organisation in the text (Persing et al., 2010; Somasundaran et al., 2014). The organisation helps readers to anticipate the upcoming textual information. Although a well-organised text is highly probable to be coherent, only the organisation does not constitute coherence. Textual organisation concerns the structural formation and logical development of a text, while lexical and semantic continuity is also indispensable for coherent text (Feng et al., 2014). Fifth, it is easier to read a coherent text than its less coherent counterpart (Garing, 2014). Thus when writing a text, it is not enough to only revise the text with careful editing and proofreading from the lexical, or grammatical aspect. Coherence aspect also should be taken into account in revising the text (Bamberg, 1983; Garing, 2014).

There are studies on computational modelling of text coherence based on the supervised learning approach, such as the Entity Grid model (Barzilay and Lapata, 2008). The Entity Grid model has been further extended into the Role Matrix model (Lin et al., 2011; Feng et al., 2014). However, these models have a few drawbacks. First,

Proceedings of TextGraphs-11: the Workshop on Graph-based Methods for Natural Language Processing, ACL 2017, pages 76–85,
Vancouver, Canada, August 3, 2017. ©2017 Association for Computational Linguistics

	department	trial	Microsoft	evidence	competitors	markets	products	brands	case	Netscape	software
S1	S	O	S	X	O	–	–	–	–	–	–
S2	–	–	O	–	–	X	S	O	–	–	–
S3	–	–	S	O	–	–	–	–	S	O	O

Table 1: Entity Grid example

Entity Grid using co-reference resolution has a bias towards the original ordering of text when comparing a text with its permutated counterparts. The co-reference resolution module is trained on well-formed texts; thus it does not perform very well for ill-organised texts. The methods utilising a discourse parser for modelling text coherence (Lin et al., 2011; Feng et al., 2014) have the same problem. Second, the supervised model often suffers from data sparsity, domain dependence, and computational cost for training. To alleviate these problems in the supervised model, Guinaudeau and Strube (2013) proposed an unsupervised coherence model known as the Entity Graph model.

The Entity Grid, Role Matrix, and Entity Graph model assumed coherence was achieved by local cohesion, i.e. repeated mentions of the same entities constitute cohesion. However, they did not capture the contribution of related-yet-not-identical entities (Petersen et al., 2015). To our best knowledge, the closest study addressing this problem was done by Li and Hovy (2014). The key idea of Li and Hovy (2014) is to learn a distributed sentence representation which captures the underlying semantic relations between consecutive sentences. To tackle these limitations of the past research, we present an unsupervised text coherence model that captures the contribution of related-yet-not-identical entities.

The rest of this paper is organised as follows. Section 2 describes related work; Section 3 introduces our proposed unsupervised method to measure text coherence from a semantic similarity perspective; Section 4 describes experimental results; then followed by the conclusion in Section 5.

2   Related work

This section provides an overview of existing coherence scoring models, both supervised and unsupervised. Entity Grid is considered as a supervised baseline in this paper. On the other hand, Entity Graph is selected as an unsupervised baseline.

s1[(The Justice Department)s is conducting an (antitrust trial)o against (Microsoft Corp.)x with (evidence)x that (the company)s is increasingly attempting to crush (competitors)o.] s2[(Microsoft)o is accused of trying to forcefully buy into (markets)x where (its own products)s are not competitive enough to unseat (established brands)o.] s3[(The case)s revolves around (evidence)o of (Microsoft)s aggressively pressuring (Netscape)o into merging (browser software)o.]

Figure 1: Part of an example text from (Barzilay and Lapata, 2008)

2.1   Entity Grid

The Entity Grid model focused on the evaluation of local cohesion developed on top of the Centering theory (Barzilay and Lapata, 2008). The key idea of the Centering theory is that the distribution of entities in coherent texts exhibits certain regularities (Grosz et al., 1995). The text is said to be less coherent if it exhibits many attention shifts, i.e. frequent changes in attention (centre) (Grosz et al., 1995). However, if the centre of attention has smooth transitions, it will be more coherent, e.g. when sentences in a text mentioning the same entity. Barzilay and Lapata (2008) proposed a computational model by representing text as a matrix called Entity Grid in which the column corresponds to entities, the row corresponds to sentences in the text, and the cell denotes the role of the entity in the sentence. The role of an entity is defined as one of S(subject), O(object), or X(neither). The cell is filled with "−" if the entity is not mentioned in the sentence. If the entity serves multiple roles in the sentence, the priority order would be S, O, and then X. They consider co-referent noun phrases as an entity. As an example, the text in Figure 1 is transformed into the Entity Grid as in Table 1. The bracketed words in Figure 1 are recognised as the entities in Table 1.

Also, they differentiate salient entities. An entity is considered salient if it occurs at least t times in the text. The text is further encoded into a feature vector, denoting the probability of local entity transitions (Barzilay and Lapata, 2008), for example the probability of bigram transition $\{S, -\}$

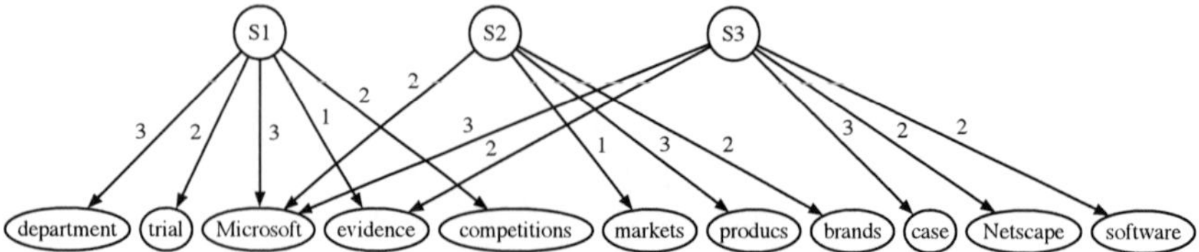

Figure 2: Example of bipartite graph

corresponding Table 1 is 2/22. As the feature vector for a text can be different with another text, the pattern of these feature vectors would reflect text coherence. Because the Entity Grid model is based on the Centering theory, it only captures the local relationship of text. Lin et al. (2011) and Feng et al. (2014) tried to tackle this limitation by filling the cell in the grid with the discourse role of the sentence in which the entity appears.

2.2 Entity Graph

To tackle the disadvantages of the supervised coherence model, Guinaudeau and Strube (2013) proposed a graph model to measure text coherence. Graph data structure allows us to relate non-adjacent sentences, spanning globally in the text to reflect global coherence as opposed to the local coherence of the Entity Grid model. A text is represented as a directed bipartite graph. The first partition is a sentence partition in which each vertex represents a sentence. The second partition is a discourse partition in which each vertex represents an entity. The weighted edge between a sentence vertex and an entity vertex is established if the entity is mentioned in the sentence. A weight is assigned to each edge based on entity's role in the sentence: 3 for a subject entity, 2 for an object entity, and 1 for others. Figure 2 shows an example of the bipartite graph transformation from the text in Figure 1.

This directed bipartite graph is further transformed into a directed projection graph in which a vertex represents a sentence, and a directed weighted edge is established between vertices if they share same entities. The direction of the edge corresponds to the surface sequential order of the sentences within the text. For example, a vertex which represents the second sentence can only have outgoing edges to third, fourth, but not to the first sentence. There are three projection methods, P_U, P_W, and P_{Acc} depending on the weighting scheme of edges. P_U assigns a binary weight to

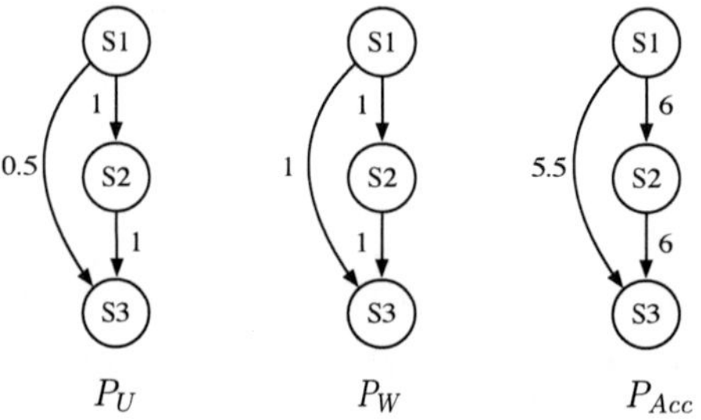

Figure 3: Example of projection graphs

each edge: one for the edge connecting two sentences sharing at least one entity in common and zero for others. P_W assigns the number of shared entities between connected sentences to each edge as its weight. P_{Acc} calculates an edge weight by accumulating the products of the weights of edges sharing an entity in the bipartite graph over the shared entities by the connected two sentences. The weight of the edge established between sentence s_i and s_j is calculated by

$$W_{ij} = \sum_{e \in E_{ij}} bw(e, s_i) \cdot bw(e, s_j), \qquad (1)$$

where E_{ij} is the set of entities shared by s_i and s_j and $bw(e, s)$ is a weight of the edge between entity e and sentence s in the bipartite graph. Furthermore, the edge weight in the projection graph can be normalised with dividing by the distance between the sentences, i.e. $|j - i|$.

Figure 3 shows the projection graph transformed from Figure 2 after the normalisation. To measure text coherence by the projection graph, Guinaudeau and Strube (2013) used the average OutDegree of every vertex in the projection graph. The OutDegree of a vertex is defined as the summation of the weight of outgoing edges leaving the vertex.

3 Constructing semantic similarity graphs

As mentioned in Section 1, a text is coherent if it can convey its communication purpose to readers, integrated as a whole, cohesive, well organised, and easy to read. We would like to approach coherence from the cohesion perspective. We argue that coherence of a text is built by cohesion among its sentences. We call our method as *Semantic Similarity Graph*.

Our proposed method employs an unsupervised learning approach. The unsupervised approach suffers less from data sparsity, domain dependence, and computational cost for training which often arise in the supervised approach. We encode a text into a graph $G(V, E)$, where V is a set of vertices and E is a set of edges in the graph. The vertex $v_i \in V$ represents the i-th sentence s_i in the text, and the weighted directed edge $e_{i,j} \in E$ represents a semantic relation from the i-th to the j-th sentences. In what follows, the term "edge" refers to the weighted directed edge.

As stated by Halliday and Hasan (1976), cohesion is a matter of lexicosemantics. Our method projects a sentence into a vector representation using pre-trained GloVe word vectors[1] by Pennington et al. (2014). A sentence consists of multiple words $\{w_1, w_2, \cdots, w_M\}$ where each of them is mapped into a vector space, i.e. $\{\vec{w}_1, \vec{w}_2, \cdots, \vec{w}_M\}$. A sentence s can be encoded as a vector $\vec{s}$ by taking the average of consisting word vectors. Formally, a sentence vector $\vec{s}$ is described as

$$\vec{s} = \frac{1}{M} \sum_{k=1}^{M} \vec{w}_k,$$

where M denotes the number of words in the sentence.

We propose three methods for constructing a graph from a text based on semantic similarity between sentence pairs in the text. Given a certain sentence vertex in the graph, how to decide its counterpart vertices for establishing edges is the crucial point. The following subsections describe each method to decide a counterpart vertex.

3.1 Preceding adjacent vertex (PAV)

People read a text from the beginning to the end and understand a particular part of the text based

---

[1] We use word vectors trained on Wikipedia 2014 + Gigaword 5, 6B tokens 400K vocab, uncased, 100d. The resource is available at https://nlp.stanford.edu/projects/glove/

```
for i ← 2 to N do
    if sim(s_i, s_{i-1}) > 0 then
        creates edge e_{i,i-1} with sim(s_i, s_{i-1}) as the weight
    else
        for j ← i - 2 to 1 do
            if sim(s_i, s_j) > 0 then
                creates edge e_{i,j} with sim(s_i, s_j) as the weight
                break
```

Figure 4: Graph construction algorithm with similarity of PAV

on information provided in the preceding part. When they do not understand a particular part, people look backwards for what they have missed. We mimic this reading process into graph construction that is reflected in the algorithm in Figure 4, where N is the number of sentences in the text to be processed.

First we define a similarity measure $\mathrm{sim}(s_i, s_j)$ of a pair of sentences s_i and s_j as

$$\mathrm{sim}(s_i, s_j) = \alpha \; \mathsf{uot}(s_i, s_j) + (1 - \alpha) \cos(\vec{s}_i, \vec{s}_j),$$

where uot is the number of unique overlapping terms between the sentences s_i and s_j divided by the number of unique terms in the two sentences; $\cos(\vec{s}_i, \vec{s}_j)$ is a cosine similarity of the sentence vectors; α is a balancing factor ranging over [0,1].

The algorithm constructs a graph by establishing a weighted directed edge from each sentence vertex to the preceding adjacent sentence vertex (PAV) if the sim value between the current and the preceding adjacent vertices exceeds zero; otherwise, the algorithm tries to establish an edge to the next closest preceding vertex with non-zero sim value. The established edge is assigned the sim value as its weight.

3.2 Single similar vertex (SSV)

Cohesion between two sentences s_i and s_j means that we need to know s_i in order to understand s_j or vice versa (Halliday and Hasan, 1976). In this sense, we interpret cohesion as a semantic dependency among sentences. We simulate the semantic dependency with the semantic similarity between sentences. Since the dependency could happen in both direction, we allow edges to the following vertices as well as preceding vertices.

In the previous method, "precedence" and "adjacency" are the important constraints for establishing the edges in graph construction. This

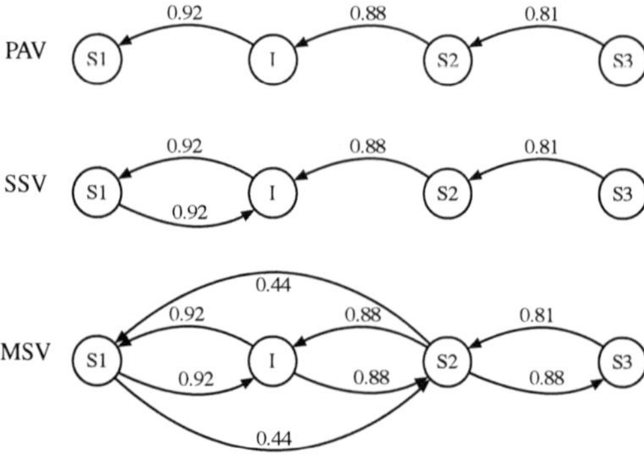

Figure 5: Example of semantic similarity graphs

method discards these constraints and establishes edges based on only the semantic similarity between sentences. However, the edges are still directed and weighted. Also, only a single outgoing edge is allowed from every vertex in the graph.

We cast semantic dependency task into an information retrieval task. When establishing an edge from a certain sentence vertex, we search for the most similar sentence in the text. The similarity measure between two sentences s_i and s_j is calculated based on the cosine similarity of their semantic vectors. An edge is established from the sentence vertex in question to the most similar sentence vertex with the weight calculated by

$$\text{weight}(e_{i,j}) = \frac{\cos(\vec{s}_i, \vec{s}_j)}{|i - j|}. \qquad (2)$$

This weight calculation takes into account the distance between two sentences, i.e. we prefer a closer counterpart.

3.3 Multiple similar vertex (MSV)

In the previous method, we allowed only a single outgoing edge for every sentence vertex in the graph. Here we discard the singular condition and allow multiple outgoing edges for every vertex. Instead of choosing the most similar sentence in the text, we choose multiple sentences that exceed a certain threshold (θ) in terms of cosine similarity with the sentence in question. Edges are established for all vertex pairs with the edge weight given in Equation (2).

Figure 5 shows an example of semantic similarity graphs constructed by three proposed methods for the text shown in Figure 6. The parameters for the PAV and MSV-based methods are the optimal value in the evaluation experiment that is de-

scribed in the next section, and the insertion sentence (I) was placed in the correct position (B).

3.4 Text coherence measure

From a constructed graph by one of the three methods explained in the preceding subsections, text coherence measure tc is calculated by averaging averaged weight of outgoing edges from every vertex in the graph as

$$tc = \frac{1}{N} \sum_{i=1}^{N} \frac{1}{L_i} \sum_{k=1}^{L_i} \text{weight}(e_{ik}),$$

where N is the number of sentences in the text and L_i is the number of outgoing edges from the vertex v_i. L_i is always one for the PAV and SSV based graph construction, since we allow only a single outgoing edge from every vertex in the graph in these methods. A larger tc value denotes a more coherent text.

The proposed models have two significant differences from the Entity Graph model, our direct competitor. First, the Entity Graph model only allows establishing outgoing edges in the following direction, i.e. from the vertex v_i to the vertex v_j, where $i < j$. On the other hand, the proposed models except for the PAV based graph construction allow edges in both directions. Second, the Entity Graph model only measures coherence based on shared entities between sentences with respect to their syntactic role. This is also the case for the Entity Grid model. The proposed models measure text coherence based on the similarity between semantic vectors of sentences; hence we can take into account related-yet-not-identical entities.

4 Evaluation and results

We evaluate the proposed methods on two experimental tasks: the document discrimination task and insertion task. All stop words are removed from the texts in this experiment, while lemmatisation is not employed.

The performance of the proposed methods is also compared with our reimplementation of Entity Grid (Barzilay and Lapata, 2008) and Entity Graph (Guinaudeau and Strube, 2013). The experimental settings for each method are described below.

PAV The balancing factor α ranges over $[0.0, 0.1, 0.2, \cdots, 1.0]$.

SSV There is no particular parameter to set.

MSV The cosine similarity threshold θ ranges over $[-1.0, 0.1, 0.2, \cdots, 0.9]$.

Entity Grid The optimal value for transition length three (bigram and trigram) is used. In document discrimination task, we implement the Entity Grid model with and without saliency. An entity is judged as salient if it is mentioned in the text at least twice. Saliency is not employed in the insertion task because the texts in the insertion task are relatively short and an entity is not mentioned many times.

Entity Graph We implemented three projection methods with normalisation: P_U, P_W, and P_{Acc}.

Co-reference resolution is not employed to avoid bias as mentioned by Nahnsen (2009). However, we follow the suggestion by Eisner and Charniak (2011) to consider all nouns (including non-head nouns) as entities in our experiment. The role of each entity is extracted using the dependency parser in Stanford CoreNLP toolkit (Manning et al., 2014).

4.1 Document discrimination task

4.1.1 Data

In the document discrimination task, sentences in a text are randomly permutated to generate another text; the task is to identify the original text given a pair of the original and the randomised one. The result is considered successful if the original is identified with the strictly higher coherence value. The performance is measured by accuracy, i.e. the ratio of successfully identified pairs to all pairs in the test set.

Our data came from a part of the English WSJ text in OntoNotes Release 5.0 (LDC2013T19). Half of the data is used for training while another half is used for testing. For each instance in both training and testing data, at most 20 random permutations were created. Detail of the data is shown in Table 2.

4.1.2 Result and discussion

Table 3 shows the result of the document discrimination task of each method with the various experimental settings.

Entity Grid without saliency performed the best (0.845), followed by Entity Grid with saliency (0.837), PAV (0.774, $\alpha = 0.4$), MSV (0.741,

	# text	# sent.	# token	# perm.
training	686	23.7	510.9	13,660
testing	683	24.4	521.4	13,586

Table 2: Data for the document discrimination task (The columns "# sent." and "# token" denote the average number of sentences and tokens in a text respectively.)

Proposed method	Setting	Accuracy
PAV	$\alpha = 0.0$	0.767
	$\alpha = 0.1$	0.771
	$\alpha = 0.2$	0.773
	$\alpha = 0.3$	0.774
	$\alpha = 0.4$	**0.774**
	$\alpha = 0.5$	0.771
	$\alpha = 0.6$	0.770
	$\alpha = 0.7$	0.766
	$\alpha = 0.8$	0.759
	$\alpha = 0.9$	0.747
	$\alpha = 1.0$	0.657
SSV		**0.676**
MSV	$\theta = -1.0$	0.741
	$\theta = 0.1$	**0.741**
	$\theta = 0.2$	0.739
	$\theta = 0.3$	0.735
	$\theta = 0.4$	0.733
	$\theta = 0.5$	0.730
	$\theta = 0.6$	0.710
	$\theta = 0.7$	0.696
	$\theta = 0.8$	0.696
	$\theta = 0.9$	0.611
Supervised baseline		
Entity Grid	w/o saliency	**0.845**
	w/ saliency	0.837
Unsupervised baseline		
Entity Graph	P_U	0.652
	P_W	0.716
	P_{Acc}	**0.725**

Table 3: Result of the document discrimination task

$\theta = 0.1$), Entity Graph (0.725), then SSV (0.676). The performances of PAV and MSV are increasing over changes of parameter until at certain point becomes steadily decreasing. We performed the McNemar test in R to find out that the difference in accuracy between every pair of methods is statistically significant at $p < 0.05$. Contrary to Barzilay and Lapata (2008), the saliency factor did not work effectively for Entity Grid in our data. The PAV and MSV based-method performed better than Entity Graph. This result suggests that coherence is not only the matter of surface overlapping of entities and their syntactic roles, but semantic similarity between sentences also should be taken into account. This also confirms that

	SSV	MSV	E-Grid	E-Graph
PAV	10,049	**11,998**	10,109	10,626
SSV	–	10,153	9,052	9,507
MSV	–	–	9,483	10,246
E-Grid	–	–	–	10,189
E-Graph	–	–	–	–

Table 4: Number of the same judgements between two methods in the document discrimination task

the semantic relation between adjacent sentences (local coherence) is more important for coherence than semantic relation between long-distance sentences in the document discrimination task.

We also calculated the number of the same judgement between all pairs of methods (questions that are answered correctly and incorrectly by both methods in the pair). Table 4 shows the number of the same judgement between every pair of the methods. We found out the PAV–MSV pair shares the largest number of the same judgement (11,998, 88.3%). The MSV-based method establishes an edge between sentences whenever their similarity exceeds the threshold. However, it has relatively many same judgements with PAV. This implies the local coherence is sufficient enough to solve the document discrimination task.

4.2 Insertion task

4.2.1 Data

In the insertion task described in Barzilay and Lapata (2008), the coherence measure is evaluated based on to what extent the measure can estimate the original sentence position in a text from which one sentence is taken out randomly. The coherence measure of the text with a taken-out sentence inserted at the original position, i.e. the original text, is expected to be the highest value among other values of text with the sentence inserted at a wrong position.

We argue, however, adopting the TOEFL® iBT insertion type question is more suitable for this kind of task than using the artificially generated texts by sentence deletion. The TOEFL® insertion type question aims at measuring test takers' ability to understand the text coherence. Test takers are given a coherent text with an *insert-sentence*. The task is to find the best place to insert the *insert-sentence*. To the best of our observation, the texts in the TOEFL® iBT insertion type question are coherent even before the *insert-sentence* is inserted. An example of the TOEFL® iBT insertion

(A) s_1[The raising of livestock is a major economic activity in semiarid lands, where grasses are generally the dominant type of natural vegetation.] (B) s_2[The consequences of an excessive number of livestock grazing in an area are the reduction of the vegetation cover and trampling and pulverization of the soil.] (C) s_3[This is usually followed by the drying of the soil and accelerated erosion.] (D)

Question:
Insert the following sentence into one of (A)-(D).
$_1$[This economic reliance on livestock in certain regions makes large tracts of land susceptible to overgrazing.]

Figure 6: Example of the TOEFL® iBT insertion type question (Education Testing Service, 2007)

type question is shown in Figure 6.

In the following evaluation, a method is judged as a success if it assigns the highest coherence value to the text formed by inserting the *insert-sentence* at the correct insertion position. We do not allow tie values and judge it as fail even though the correct position has the highest tie value.

We collected 104 insertion type questions from various TOEFL® iBT preparation books. The average number of sentences in a text is 7.05 (SD: standard deviation=1.85); the average number of tokens in a text is 139.8 (SD=43.7). As the data size is relatively small, we adopted the one-held-out cross validation for the Entity Grid model. The same rank is assigned to incorrect insertion positions when training the Entity Grid model. We did not adopt the Entity Grid model considering saliency since each text is relatively short in this data thus term frequency (saliency) tends to be low for all terms.

4.2.2 Result and discussion

Table 5 shows the result of the insertion task of each method with the various experimental settings. Our proposed methods showed good performance, particularly the PAV-based graph construction method outperformed both baselines: Entity Grid and Entity Graph. The PAV method obtained the best performance at $\alpha = 0.0$, while MSV method performed best at $\theta = 0.8$. However, the McNemar test revealed that the difference in accuracy between every pair of methods was not statistically significant at $p < 0.05$. This is probably due to the limited size of the insertion data compared with the document discrimination task.

There are two questions correctly answered and 31 questions incorrectly answered by all methods. These two correctly answered questions have

Proposed method	Setting	Accuracy
PAV	$\alpha = 0.0$	**0.356**
	$\alpha = 0.1$	0.337
	$\alpha = 0.2$	0.327
	$\alpha = 0.3$	0.327
	$\alpha = 0.4$	0.317
	$\alpha = 0.5$	0.327
	$\alpha = 0.6$	0.308
	$\alpha = 0.7$	0.279
	$\alpha = 0.8$	0.317
	$\alpha = 0.9$	0.337
	$\alpha = 1.0$	0.212
SSV		**0.346**
MSV	$\theta = -1.0$	0.298
	$\theta = 0.1$	0.298
	$\theta = 0.2$	0.298
	$\theta = 0.3$	0.298
	$\theta = 0.4$	0.298
	$\theta = 0.5$	0.279
	$\theta = 0.6$	0.269
	$\theta = 0.7$	0.317
	$\theta = 0.8$	**0.327**
	$\theta = 0.9$	0.067
Supervised baseline		
Entity Grid	w/o saliency	**0.346**
Unsupervised baseline		
Entity Graph	P_U	0.192
	P_W	0.222
	P_{Acc}	**0.260**

Table 5: Result of the insertion task

similar characteristics, having word overlaps and synonyms across adjacent sentences. These questions also tend to contain more common words. On the other hand, the failed questions tend to contain more uncommon words, technical terms and named entities. Although the successful questions also contain named entities, they were mentioned more frequently in the texts as opposed to the failed questions. Therefore we suspected the limited coverage of our GloVe dictionary and investigated the proportion of the out of vocabulary (OOV) ratio of the texts. Among all of the questions, there are 32 out of 104 questions including the OOV words; each question contains one to three OOV words in type/in token. All methods failed in 15 out of these 32 questions but succeeded in the rest 17. This fact suggests that OOV words are not necessarily the main reason for failures in the insertion task.

Comparing the parameters (α of PAV and θ of MSV) in Table 3 and Table 5, they are different to achieve the best performance in two different datasets. In the PAV-based method, there is no significant difference in the average uot value of

every pair of adjacent two sentences between the datasets. We also calculated the cosine similarity of every pair of adjacent two sentences to find more similar adjacent sentences in the insertion task data than in the document discrimination task data; 90% of the adjacent sentence similarities lies in $0.3 \sim 0.6$ in the document discrimination task, while it ranges $0.5 \sim 0.9$ in the insertion task data. This difference suggests that the uot factor helps relatively more in the document discrimination task for the PAV-based method, while it has less impact in the insertion task. This explains the difference α values of PAV across the two tasks.

To investigate the difference of the parameter θ in the MSV-based model, we calculated the cosine similarity of every sentence pair in the text. In both datasets, more than 90% of the sentence similarities lies in $0.5 \sim 1.0$. When the similarity is transformed into the edge weight by dividing by the sentence distance, the difference becomes apparent; while 86.6% of the edge weights in the document discrimination task lies less than 0.2, the edge weights scatter over $0 \sim 1.0$ in the insertion task. This happens because the average length of the texts in the document discrimination task is longer than that of the insertion task. Unless setting a low threshold (θ), the MSV-based model hardly establishes edges between sentence vertices. In other words, establishing edges between distant sentences would contribute to the performance of these tasks.

	SSV	MSV	E-Grid	E-Graph
PAV	75	79	57	66
SSV	–	**84**	58	67
MSV	–	–	54	65
E-Grid	–	–	–	69
E-Graph	–	–	–	–

Table 6: Number of the same answers between two methods in the insertion task

Table 6 shows the number of the same answers between every pair of the methods. The SSV–MSV pair shares the most same answers in the insertion task among all pairs (84, 80.8%), followed by the PAV–MSV pair (79, 76.0%), then PAV–SSV pair (75, 72.1%). The PAV-based method performs best without considering the overlapping terms between the adjacent sentences (uot) by setting $\alpha = 0$. In this case, the PAV-based method is almost similar to the SSV-based method except for allowing only backwards edges. However, Table 6 shows the PAV-based method answered differently from the SSV-based method in almost 30% questions. To further investigate the difference, we focused on the questions that were answered incorrectly by the PAV-based method but answered correctly by the SSV-based method. There are 14 of such questions, in which the SSV-based method tends to establish edges between distant sentences; the average distance between sentence vertices is 2.8 ($SD = 0.7$). This suggests that the SSV-based method could capture distant sentence relations contributing to text coherence more appropriately than the PAV-based method.

We also investigated 11 questions that were answered incorrectly by the PAV-based method but answered correctly by the MSV-based method. In these questions, the MSV-based method tends to establish more edges than the PAV-based method. The average number of outgoing edges from a sentence vertex in the graph constructed by the MSV-based method is 2.5 ($SD = 1.8$). In addition, the MSV-based method tends to establish edges between distant sentences as well as the SSV-based method; the average distance between sentence vertices is 2.6 ($SD = 0.9$). This suggests that the MSV-based method also could capture many distant sentence relations contributing to text coherence more appropriately than the PAV-based method.

Although the PAV-based method performs best with the present data, which considers only local cohesion between adjacent sentences, we need to introduce a more refined mechanism for incorporating distant sentence relations than the current SSV and MSV-based methods, as we showed that long-distance relations could contribute in determining text coherence. The representation of sentences and calculation of similarity between sentences would be direct targets of the refinement.

5 Conclusion

This paper presented three novel unsupervised text coherence scoring methods, in which text coherence is regarded to be realised by cohesion of sentences in the text and the cohesion is represented in a graph structure corresponding to the text. In the graph structure, a vertex corresponds to a sentence in the text, and an edge represents a semantic relationship between corresponding sentences. As cohesion is a matter of lexicosemantics, sentences are transformed into semantic vector representa-

tions, and their similarity is calculated based on the cosine similarity between the vectors. Edges between sentence vertices are established based on the similarity and distance between the sentences. We presented three methods to construct a graph: the PAV, SSV, and MSV-based methods.

We evaluated the proposed methods in the document discrimination task and the insertion task. Our best performing method (PAV) outperformed the unsupervised baseline (Entity Graph) but not the supervised baseline (Entity Grid) in the document discrimination task. The difference was statistically significant at $p < 0.05$. In the insertion task, our best performing method (PAV) outperformed both supervised and unsupervised baselines, but the difference is not statistically significant at $p < 0.05$. We argue that further experiment is necessary with a larger size of data in the insertion task.

Our experimental result showed that our best proposed method (PAV) performed 0.774 in accuracy in the document discrimination task, but only performed 0.356 in the insertion task. There is a big gap in their performance between two tasks. The error analysis revealed a possibility to improve the performance by introducing a more refined representation of sentence vectors and calculation in semantic the similarity between sentences for capturing distant relations between sentences.

References

Betty Bamberg. 1983. What makes a text coherent. *College Composition and Communication* 34(4):417–429.

Regina Barzilay and Mirela Lapata. 2008. Modeling local coherence: Entity based approach. *Computational Linguistics* 34(1):1–34.

Education Testing Service. 2007. *The Official Guide to the New TOEFL® iBT International Edition*. Mc-Graw Hill, Singapore.

Micha Eisner and Eugene Charniak. 2011. Extending the entity grid with entity-specific features. In *Proceedings of the 49th Annual Meeting of the Association for Computational Linguistics: Human Language Technologies: Short Papers - Volume 2*. Association for Computational Linguistics, Stroudsburg, PA, USA, HLT '11, pages 125–129. http://dl.acm.org/citation.cfm?id=2002736.2002764.

Vanessa Wei Feng, Ziheng Lin, and Graeme Hirst. 2014. The impact of deep hierarchical discourse structures in the evaluation of text coherence. In *Proceedings of COLING 2014, the 25th International Conference on Computational Linguistics: Technical Papers*. Dublin City University and Association for Computational Linguistics, Dublin, Ireland, pages 940–949. http://www.aclweb.org/anthology/C14-1089.

Alphie G. Garing. 2014. Coherence in argumentative essays of first year college of liberal arts students at de la salle university. *DLSU Research Congress* .

Barbara J. Grosz and Candace L. Sidner. 1986. Attention, intentions, and the structure of discourse. *Computational Linguistics* 12(3):175–204. http://dl.acm.org/citation.cfm?id=12457.12458.

Barbara J. Grosz, Scott Weinstein, and Aravind K. Joshi. 1995. Centering: A framework for modeling the local coherence of discourse. *Computational Linguistics* 21(2):203–225. http://dl.acm.org/citation.cfm?id=211190.211198.

Camille Guinaudeau and Michael Strube. 2013. Graph-based local coherence modeling. In *Proceedings of the 51st Annual Meeting of the Association for Computational Linguistics (Volume 1: Long Papers)*. Association for Computational Linguistics, Sofia, Bulgaria, pages 93–103. http://www.aclweb.org/anthology/P13-1010.

M.A.K Halliday and Ruqaiya Hasan. 1976. *Cohesion in English*. Longman, Singapore.

Jiwei Li and Eduard Hovy. 2014. A model of coherence based on distributed sentence representation. In *Proceedings of the 2014 Conference on Empirical Methods in Natural Language Processing (EMNLP)*. Association for Computational Linguistics, Doha, Qatar, pages 2039–2048. http://www.aclweb.org/anthology/D14-1218.

Ziheng Lin, Hwee Tou Ng, and Min-Yen Kan. 2011. Automatically evaluating text coherence using discourse relations. In *Proceedings of the 49th Annual Meeting of the Association for Computational Linguistics: Human Language Technologies*. Association for Computational Linguistics, Portland, Oregon, USA, pages 997–1006. http://www.aclweb.org/anthology/P11-1100.

William C. Mann and Sandra A. Thompson. 1988. Rhetorical structure theory: Toward a functional theory of text organization. *Text* 8(3):243–281.

Christopher Manning, Mihai Surdeanu, John Bauer, Jenny Finkel, Steven Bethard, and David McClosky. 2014. The stanford corenlp natural language processing toolkit. In *Proceedings of 52nd Annual Meeting of the Association for Computational Linguistics: System Demonstrations*. Association for Computational Linguistics, Baltimore, Maryland, pages 55–60. http://www.aclweb.org/anthology/P14-5010.

Thade Nahnsen. 2009. Domain-independent shallow sentence ordering. In *Proceedings of Human Language Technologies: The 2009 Annual Conference of the North American Chapter of the Association for Computational Linguistics, Companion Volume: Student Research Workshop and Doctoral Consortium*. Association for Computational Linguistics, Boulder, Colorado, pages 78–83. http://www.aclweb.org/anthology/N/N09/N09-3014.

Jeffrey Pennington, Richard Socher, and Christopher Manning. 2014. Glove: Global vectors for word representation. In *Proceedings of the 2014 Conference on Empirical Methods in Natural Language Processing (EMNLP)*. Association for Computational Linguistics, Doha, Qatar, pages 1532–1543. http://www.aclweb.org/anthology/D14-1162.

Isaac Persing, Alan Davis, and Vincent Ng. 2010. Modeling organization in student essays. In *Proceedings of the 2010 Conference on Empirical Methods in Natural Language Processing*. Association for Computational Linguistics, Cambridge, MA, pages 229–239. http://www.aclweb.org/anthology/D10-1023.

Casper Petersen, Christina Lioma, Jakob Grue Simonsen, and Birger Larsen. 2015. Entropy and graph based modelling of document coherence using discourse entities: An application to ir. In *Proceedings of the 2015 International Conference on The Theory of Information Retrieval*. ACM, New York, NY, USA, ICTIR '15, pages 191–200. https://doi.org/10.1145/2808194.2809458.

Swapna Somasundaran, Jill Burstein, and Martin Chodorow. 2014. Lexical chaining for measuring discourse coherence quality in test-taker essays. In *Proceedings of COLING 2014, the 25th International Conference on Computational Linguistics: Technical Papers*. Dublin City University and Association for Computational Linguistics, Dublin, Ireland, pages 950–961. http://www.aclweb.org/anthology/C14-1090.

Amalia Todirascu, Thomas Francois, Delphine Bernhard, Nuria Gala, and Anne-Laure Ligozat. 2016. Are cohesive features relevant for text readability evaluation? In *Proceedings of COLING 2016, the 26th International Conference on Computational Linguistics: Technical Papers*. The COLING 2016 Organizing Committee, Osaka, Japan, pages 987–997. http://aclweb.org/anthology/C16-1094.

Florian Wolf and Edward Gibson. 2005. Representing discourse coherence: A corpus-based study. *Computational Linguistics* 31(2):249–288. https://doi.org/10.1162/0891201054223977.

Author Index

Association for Computational Linguistics
209 N. Eighth Street
Stroudsburg, Pennsylvania 18360

CURRAN ASSOCIATES INC.
proceedings
.com

ISBN 978-1-5108-4574-9